Magic: A Very Short Introduction

VERY SHORT INTRODUCTIONS are for anyone wanting a stimulating and accessible way in to a new subject. They are written by experts, and have been published in more than 25 languages worldwide.

The series began in 1995, and now represents a wide variety of topics in history, philosophy, religion, science, and the humanities. The VSI library now contains 300 volumes—a Very Short Introduction to everything from ancient Egypt and Indian philosophy to conceptual art and cosmology—and will continue to grow in a variety of disciplines.

Very Short Introductions available now:

ADVERTISING Winston Fletcher
AFRICAN HISTORY John Parker and Richard Rathbone
AGNOSTICISM Robin Le Poidevin
AMERICAN IMMIGRATION David A. Gerber
AMERICAN POLITICAL PARTIES AND ELECTIONS L. Sandy Maisel
THE AMERICAN PRESIDENCY Charles O. Jones
ANARCHISM Colin Ward
ANCIENT EGYPT Ian Shaw
ANCIENT GREECE Paul Cartledge
ANCIENT PHILOSOPHY Julia Annas
ANCIENT WARFARE Harry Sidebottom
ANGELS David Albert Jones
ANGLICANISM Mark Chapman
THE ANGLO-SAXON AGE John Blair
THE ANIMAL KINGDOM Peter Holland
ANIMAL RIGHTS David DeGrazia
ANTISEMITISM Steven Beller
THE APOCRYPHAL GOSPELS Paul Foster
ARCHAEOLOGY Paul Bahn
ARCHITECTURE Andrew Ballantyne
ARISTOCRACY William Doyle
ARISTOTLE Jonathan Barnes
ART HISTORY Dana Arnold
ART THEORY Cynthia Freeland
ATHEISM Julian Baggini
AUGUSTINE Henry Chadwick
AUTISM Uta Frith
BARTHES Jonathan Culler
BEAUTY Roger Scruton
BESTSELLERS John Sutherland
THE BIBLE John Riches
BIBLICAL ARCHAEOLOGY Eric H. Cline
BIOGRAPHY Hermione Lee
THE BLUES Elijah Wald
THE BOOK OF MORMON Terryl Givens
THE BRAIN Michael O'Shea
BRITISH POLITICS Anthony Wright
BUDDHA Michael Carrithers
BUDDHISM Damien Keown
BUDDHIST ETHICS Damien Keown
CANCER Nicholas James
CAPITALISM James Fulcher
CATHOLICISM Gerald O'Collins
THE CELL Terence Allen and Graham Cowling
THE CELTS Barry Cunliffe
CHAOS Leonard Smith
CHILDREN'S LITERATURE Kimberley Reynolds
CHOICE THEORY Michael Allingham
CHRISTIAN ART Beth Williamson
CHRISTIAN ETHICS D. Stephen Long
CHRISTIANITY Linda Woodhead
CITIZENSHIP Richard Bellamy
CLASSICAL MYTHOLOGY Helen Morales
CLASSICS Mary Beard and John Henderson
CLAUSEWITZ Michael Howard
THE COLD WAR Robert McMahon

COLONIAL LATIN AMERICAN LITERATURE Rolena Adorno
COMMUNISM Leslie Holmes
THE COMPUTER Darrel Ince
CONSCIENCE Paul Strohm
CONSCIOUSNESS Susan Blackmore
CONTEMPORARY ART Julian Stallabrass
CONTINENTAL PHILOSOPHY Simon Critchley
COSMOLOGY Peter Coles
CRITICAL THEORY Stephen Eric Bronner
THE CRUSADES Christopher Tyerman
CRYPTOGRAPHY Fred Piper and Sean Murphy
DADA AND SURREALISM David Hopkins
DARWIN Jonathan Howard
THE DEAD SEA SCROLLS Timothy Lim
DEMOCRACY Bernard Crick
DERRIDA Simon Glendinning
DESCARTES Tom Sorell
DESERTS Nick Middleton
DESIGN John Heskett
DEVELOPMENTAL BIOLOGY Lewis Wolpert
DICTIONARIES Lynda Mugglestone
DINOSAURS David Norman
DIPLOMACY Joseph M. Siracusa
DOCUMENTARY FILM Patricia Aufderheide
DREAMING J. Allan Hobson
DRUGS Leslie Iversen
DRUIDS Barry Cunliffe
EARLY MUSIC Thomas Forrest Kelly
THE EARTH Martin Redfern
ECONOMICS Partha Dasgupta
EGYPTIAN MYTH Geraldine Pinch
EIGHTEENTH-CENTURY BRITAIN Paul Langford
THE ELEMENTS Philip Ball
EMOTION Dylan Evans
EMPIRE Stephen Howe
ENGELS Terrell Carver
ENGLISH LITERATURE Jonathan Bate
ENVIRONMENTAL ECONOMICS Stephen Smith
EPIDEMIOLOGY Rodolfo Saracci
ETHICS Simon Blackburn
THE EUROPEAN UNION John Pinder and Simon Usherwood
EVOLUTION Brian and Deborah Charlesworth
EXISTENTIALISM Thomas Flynn
FASCISM Kevin Passmore
FASHION Rebecca Arnold
FEMINISM Margaret Walters
FILM MUSIC Kathryn Kalinak
THE FIRST WORLD WAR Michael Howard
FOLK MUSIC Mark Slobin
FORENSIC PSYCHOLOGY David Canter
FORENSIC SCIENCE Jim Fraser
FOSSILS Keith Thomson
FOUCAULT Gary Gutting
FREE SPEECH Nigel Warburton
FREE WILL Thomas Pink
FRENCH LITERATURE John D. Lyons
THE FRENCH REVOLUTION William Doyle
FREUD Anthony Storr
FUNDAMENTALISM Malise Ruthven
GALAXIES John Gribbin
GALILEO Stillman Drake
GAME THEORY Ken Binmore
GANDHI Bhikhu Parekh
GENIUS Andrew Robinson
GEOGRAPHY John Matthews and David Herbert
GEOPOLITICS Klaus Dodds
GERMAN LITERATURE Nicholas Boyle
GERMAN PHILOSOPHY Andrew Bowie
GLOBAL CATASTROPHES Bill McGuire
GLOBAL ECONOMIC HISTORY Robert C. Allen
GLOBAL WARMING Mark Maslin
GLOBALIZATION Manfred Steger
THE GREAT DEPRESSION AND THE NEW DEAL Eric Rauchway
HABERMAS James Gordon Finlayson
HEGEL Peter Singer
HEIDEGGER Michael Inwood
HERODOTUS Jennifer T. Roberts
HIEROGLYPHS Penelope Wilson
HINDUISM Kim Knott
HISTORY John H. Arnold

THE HISTORY OF ASTRONOMY Michael Hoskin
THE HISTORY OF LIFE Michael Benton
THE HISTORY OF MEDICINE William Bynum
THE HISTORY OF TIME Leofranc Holford-Strevens
HIV/AIDS Alan Whiteside
HOBBES Richard Tuck
HUMAN EVOLUTION Bernard Wood
HUMAN RIGHTS Andrew Clapham
HUMANISM Stephen Law
HUME A. J. Ayer
IDEOLOGY Michael Freeden
INDIAN PHILOSOPHY Sue Hamilton
INFORMATION Luciano Floridi
INNOVATION Mark Dodgson and David Gann
INTELLIGENCE Ian J. Deary
INTERNATIONAL MIGRATION Khalid Koser
INTERNATIONAL RELATIONS Paul Wilkinson
ISLAM Malise Ruthven
ISLAMIC HISTORY Adam Silverstein
JESUS Richard Bauckham
JOURNALISM Ian Hargreaves
JUDAISM Norman Solomon
JUNG Anthony Stevens
KABBALAH Joseph Dan
KAFKA Ritchie Robertson
KANT Roger Scruton
KEYNES Robert Skidelsky
KIERKEGAARD Patrick Gardiner
THE KORAN Michael Cook
LANDSCAPES AND GEOMORPHOLOGY Andrew Goudie and Heather Viles
LATE ANTIQUITY Gillian Clark
LAW Raymond Wacks
THE LAWS OF THERMODYNAMICS Peter Atkins
LEADERSHIP Keith Grint
LINCOLN Allen C. Guelzo
LINGUISTICS Peter Matthews
LITERARY THEORY Jonathan Culler
LOCKE John Dunn
LOGIC Graham Priest
MACHIAVELLI Quentin Skinner
MADNESS Andrew Scull
MAGIC Owen Davies
THE MARQUIS DE SADE John Phillips
MARTIN LUTHER Scott H. Hendrix
MARX Peter Singer
MATHEMATICS Timothy Gowers
THE MEANING OF LIFE Terry Eagleton
MEDICAL ETHICS Tony Hope
MEDIEVAL BRITAIN John Gillingham and Ralph A. Griffiths
MEMORY Jonathan K. Foster
MICHAEL FARADAY Frank A. J. L. James
MODERN ART David Cottington
MODERN CHINA Rana Mitter
MODERN FRANCE Vanessa Schwartz
MODERN IRELAND Senia Pašeta
MODERN JAPAN Christopher Goto-Jones
MODERNISM Christopher Butler
MOLECULES Philip Ball
MORMONISM Richard Lyman Bushman
MUHAMMAD Jonathan A. C. Brown
MULTICULTURALISM Ali Rattansi
MUSIC Nicholas Cook
MYTH Robert A. Segal
NATIONALISM Steven Grosby
NELSON MANDELA Elleke Boehmer
NEOLIBERALISM Manfred Steger and Ravi Roy
THE NEW TESTAMENT Luke Timothy Johnson
THE NEW TESTAMENT AS LITERATURE Kyle Keefer
NEWTON Robert Iliffe
NIETZSCHE Michael Tanner
NINETEENTH-CENTURY BRITAIN Christopher Harvie and H. C. G. Matthew
THE NORMAN CONQUEST George Garnett
NORTH AMERICAN INDIANS Theda Perdue and Michael D. Green
NORTHERN IRELAND Marc Mulholland
NOTHING Frank Close
NUCLEAR POWER Maxwell Irvine

NUCLEAR WEAPONS
Joseph M. Siracusa
NUMBERS Peter M. Higgins
THE OLD TESTAMENT
Michael D. Coogan
ORGANIZATIONS Mary Jo Hatch
PAGANISM Owen Davies
PARTICLE PHYSICS Frank Close
PAUL E. P. Sanders
PENTECOSTALISM William K. Kay
THE PERIODIC TABLE Eric R. Scerri
PHILOSOPHY Edward Craig
PHILOSOPHY OF LAW
Raymond Wacks
PHILOSOPHY OF SCIENCE
Samir Okasha
PHOTOGRAPHY Steve Edwards
PLANETS David A. Rothery
PLATO Julia Annas
POLITICAL PHILOSOPHY
David Miller
POLITICS Kenneth Minogue
POSTCOLONIALISM Robert Young
POSTMODERNISM Christopher Butler
POSTSTRUCTURALISM
Catherine Belsey
PREHISTORY Chris Gosden
PRESOCRATIC PHILOSOPHY
Catherine Osborne
PRIVACY Raymond Wacks
PROGRESSIVISM Walter Nugent
PROTESTANTISM Mark A. Noll
PSYCHIATRY Tom Burns
PSYCHOLOGY
Gillian Butler and Freda McManus
PURITANISM Francis J. Bremer
THE QUAKERS Pink Dandelion
QUANTUM THEORY
John Polkinghorne
RACISM Ali Rattansi
THE REAGAN REVOLUTION
Gil Troy
REALITY Jan Westerhoff
THE REFORMATION Peter Marshall
RELATIVITY Russell Stannard
RELIGION IN AMERICA Timothy Beal
THE RENAISSANCE Jerry Brotton
RENAISSANCE ART
Geraldine A. Johnson
RISK Baruch Fischhoff and John Kadvany
ROMAN BRITAIN Peter Salway
THE ROMAN EMPIRE
Christopher Kelly
ROMANTICISM Michael Ferber
ROUSSEAU Robert Wokler
RUSSELL A. C. Grayling
RUSSIAN LITERATURE Catriona Kelly
THE RUSSIAN REVOLUTION
S. A. Smith
SCHIZOPHRENIA
Chris Frith and Eve Johnstone
SCHOPENHAUER Christopher Janaway
SCIENCE AND RELIGION
Thomas Dixon
SCIENCE FICTION David Seed
THE SCIENTIFIC REVOLUTION
Lawrence M. Principe
SCOTLAND Rab Houston
SEXUALITY Véronique Mottier
SHAKESPEARE Germaine Greer
SIKHISM Eleanor Nesbitt
SLEEP
Steven W. Lockley and Russell G. Foster
SOCIAL AND CULTURAL
ANTHROPOLOGY
John Monaghan and Peter Just
SOCIALISM Michael Newman
SOCIOLOGY Steve Bruce
SOCRATES C. C. W. Taylor
THE SOVIET UNION Stephen Lovell
THE SPANISH CIVIL WAR
Helen Graham
SPANISH LITERATURE Jo Labanyi
SPINOZA Roger Scruton
STATISTICS David J. Hand
STUART BRITAIN John Morrill
SUPERCONDUCTIVITY
Stephen Blundell
TERRORISM Charles Townshend
THEOLOGY David F. Ford
THOMAS AQUINAS Fergus Kerr
TOCQUEVILLE Harvey C. Mansfield
TRAGEDY Adrian Poole
THE TUDORS John Guy
TWENTIETH-CENTURY BRITAIN
Kenneth O. Morgan
THE UNITED NATIONS
Jussi M. Hanhimäki
THE U.S. CONGRESS
Donald A. Ritchie

UTOPIANISM Lyman Tower Sargent
THE VIKINGS Julian Richards
VIRUSES Dorothy H. Crawford
WITCHCRAFT Malcolm Gaskill
WITTGENSTEIN A. C. Grayling
WORLD MUSIC Philip Bohlman
THE WORLD TRADE ORGANIZATION Amrita Narlikar
WRITING AND SCRIPT Andrew Robinson

Available soon:

THE AZTECS David Carrasco
THE CULTURAL REVOLUTION Richard Curt Kraus
FILM Michael Wood
ITALIAN LITERATURE Peter Hainsworth and David Robey
STEM CELLS Jonathan Slack

For more information visit our website
www.oup.com/vsi/

Owen Davies

MAGIC

A Very Short Introduction

OXFORD
UNIVERSITY PRESS

Great Clarendon Street, Oxford OX2 6DP

Oxford University Press is a department of the University of Oxford.
It furthers the University's objective of excellence in research, scholarship,
and education by publishing worldwide in

Oxford New York

Auckland Cape Town Dar es Salaam Hong Kong Karachi
Kuala Lumpur Madrid Melbourne Mexico City Nairobi
New Delhi Shanghai Taipei Toronto

With offices in

Argentina Austria Brazil Chile Czech Republic France Greece
Guatemala Hungary Italy Japan Poland Portugal Singapore
South Korea Switzerland Thailand Turkey Ukraine Vietnam

Oxford is a registered trade mark of Oxford University Press
in the UK and in certain other countries

Published in the United States
by Oxford University Press Inc., New York

First published 2012

British Library Cataloguing in Publication Data
Data available

Library of Congress Cataloging in Publication Data
Data available

Typeset by SPI Publisher Services, Pondicherry, India

Printed and bound by
CPI Group (UK) Ltd, Croydon, CR0 4YY

ISBN 978-0-19-958802-2

Contents

List of illustrations xi

Introduction: initial observations 1

1 Anthropologies of magic 14

2 Historical perspectives 32

3 All in the mind? 49

4 Writing magic 66

5 Practising magic 82

6 Magic and the modern world 99

Final thoughts 113

References 114

Further reading 129

Index 131

List of illustrations

1 A Senegalise marabout at work **10**
© Robert Harding Picture Library Ltd/Alamy

2 Bronisław Malinowski encountering a Trobriander 'sorcerer' **23**
© Mary Evans Picture Library

3 'Sorcerer' from Binsa **24**
© Wellcome Library, London

4 A mesmerist and his patient **38**
© Wellcome Library, London

5 Medieval juggler, from 11th-century French manuscript **52**
© 2011 The British Library Board

6 *Une leçon clinique à la Salpêtrière* (1887), by André Brouillet: Charcot demonstrating hysteria **60**
© Faculty of Medicine, Lyon/The Bridgeman Art Library

7 Malayan curse in the language of the djinns **76**
© Wellcome Library, London

8 Syrian amulet, silver hand bearing Hebraic characters **77**
© Pitt Rivers Museum, University of Oxford

9 Terracotta figurine pierced by 13 nails, from 3rd- or 4th-century Egypt **84**
© Genevra Kornbluth

10 Witch bottle found buried in King's Lynn, Norfolk, in 1905 **96**
© Norwich Castle Museum and Art Gallery

11 'The Incantation' (1901), photograph by John Cimon Warburg **102**
© National Media Museum/SSPL

Introduction: initial observations

Defining 'magic' is a maddening task. Over the last century, numerous philosophers, anthropologists, historians, and theologians have attempted to pin down its essential meaning, sometimes analysing it in such complex and abstruse depth that it all but loses its sense altogether. For this reason, many of those researching the *practice* of magic in the past and present often shy away from providing a detailed definition, assuming their readers understand it to pertain generally to human control of supernatural forces. Away from the scholarly world, 'magic' continues to pervade popular imagination and idiom. People feel comfortable with its contemporary multiple meanings, unaware of the controversy, conflict, and debate its definition has caused over two and a half millennia. In common usage today, 'magic' is uttered in reference to the supernatural, superstition, illusion, trickery, miracles, fantasies, and as a simple superlative. We talk of the 'magic of cinema'. The literary genre known as 'magical realism' has considerable appeal. Modern scientists have ironically incorporated the word into their vocabulary, with their 'magic acid', 'magic bullets', and 'magic angles'.

Since the European Enlightenment, magic has often been seen as a marker of primitivism, of a benighted earlier stage of human development. Yet across the modern globalized world, hundreds of millions continue to resort to magic – and also to fear it. Magic provides explanations and remedies for those living in extreme poverty and without access to alternatives. In the industrial West, with its state welfare systems, religious fundamentalists decry the continued moral threat posed by magic. Nevertheless, under the guise of neopaganism, its practice has become a religion in itself. Magic continues to be a truly global issue.

Every definition is a product of its time. Words and concepts accrue multiple meanings, change meaning and lose meaning depending on the social, cultural, religious, and intellectual development of the societies that use them. As we shall see, 'magic' provides a valuable vehicle for exploring these relationships. This *Very Short Introduction* does not attempt to provide a concluding definition of magic; it is beyond simple definition. Instead, it explores the many ways in which magic, as an idea and a practice, has been understood and employed over the millennia.

Terminology

Magic derives from the Greek *mageia*, which in its earliest definition referred to the ceremonies and rituals performed by a *magos* (plural *magoi*). The *magoi*, or magi, were said to be priest-magicians from the East, from Chaldea, a Babylonian kingdom in southern Iraq, or Persia, now Iran. Indeed, *magos* ultimately derives from the Persian *makuš*. For the ancient Greeks, then, *mageia* was foreign. The Greeks had other terms to describe magic. There was *nekuomanteia* (necromancy) for the act of communication with the dead for prophetic purposes; *pharmaka* for the spells, drugs, and poisons employed by sorcerers or witches; *goētes* for 'sorcerers' who were masters of illusion and casters of spells. Allocating distinct magical crafts to each term is not straightforward in an ancient Greek context, though. In some sources, *mageia* was used interchangeably with *goeteia* (the practices of *goētes*) and *pharmaka*. So in the 5th century BCE, *mageia* was not the general all-embracing term for magical practices it came to be during the Roman era.

Most of what we know of the *magoi* derives from 5th- and 4th-century BCE Greek sources that are generally hostile to their foreign brand of religion. Sophocles refers to a *magos* as a 'crafty begging priest', while another source refers to the 'tricks of *magoi*'. They are described as officiating over human and animal sacrifices, commanding the spirits of the dead, and healing the sick. According to the 5th-century BCE historian Herodotus, they officiated over libations and interpreted dreams and solar eclipses. They sang hymns and incantations to the gods at sunrise. Their practices were distinct from those of the Greek priesthood in several respects. The *magoi* used libations of milk whereas the Greeks generally did not, for example, and it is thought that they whispered or sang their hymns and rituals in a low voice – a suspicious practice. Furthermore, they were thought to practise incest.

The principal religion of 5th-century BCE Persia was Zoroastrianism – in antiquity one of the largest religions, but today one of the smallest of the surviving ancient theologies. Zoroaster was a fabled prophet who preached the divine authority of the supreme being Ahura Mazda, the source of all goodness who will eventually prevail over the forces of chaos and evil in the world. The first Greek references to Zoroaster do not explicitly link the *magoi* to him, but the relationship is concrete by the 4th century. Described as fire worshippers, Zorastrians, past and present, did not actually *worship* fire as such, but rather saw it as representing Ahura Mazda's wisdom. If the early Greek statements are true regarding wandering or begging priests, then Persian *magoi* set out to spread their faith or practices westwards. They were certainly associated with the Persian advance into Greek territory by King Xerxes in the 480s, and they later stood accused of infecting the Hellenic world with magic. Then again, rumours also abounded in the Roman world that some of Greece's leading thinkers had set off eastwards to learn from the *magoi*.

During the Roman period, the definition of *mageia* or *magia* broadened. It was no longer seen primarily in terms of the activities of a foreign priesthood, a mystery cult. One of the first illustrations of this shift is found in the writings of the Roman naturalist Pliny the Elder (23–79 CE). In his *Naturalis historia*, he discussed at length a wide range of beliefs and practices labelled as 'magical vanities', whose efficacy he dismissed, and the origins of which he frequently attributed to the Persians. To give you a flavour of them, here is Pliny's description of some magicians' amulets against fever:

> the wasp known by the name of 'pseudosphex', which is always to be seen flying alone, caught with the left hand and attached beneath the patient's chin. Some use for this purpose the first wasp that a person sees in that year. Other amulets are, a viper's head, severed from the body and wrapped in a linen cloth; a viper's heart, removed from the reptile while still alive; the snout of a mouse and the tips of its ears, wrapped in red cloth.

It was also in the Roman period that *magos* began to be applied to females.

Around the time Pliny was writing his *Natural History*, the first New Testament texts were being written down, and with them the story of how magi bearing gifts from the East followed a star that led them to the infant Jesus. The way the Church Fathers interpreted the magi story became part of the broader process whereby the early Church attempted to 'demagify' the New Testament, and thereby create a fundamental division between magic and religion. So the idea that astrology had led the magi to their destiny was obviously problematic. Tertullian of Carthage (*c.* 160–220 CE) asked, 'What then? Shall therefore the religion of those Magi act as patrons now also to astrologers?' The answer was no, for as he and other Church Fathers explained, any demonic or 'superstitious' powers the magi possessed were dispelled by the shining star and sacred purpose of their journey.

Origen, a contemporary of Tertullian, accepted the magi were astrologers but it was not this false science that had led them to Christ. They were guided, instead, by their interpretation of a prophecy made by the Old Testament pagan prophet Balaam that a star would come forth from Jacob, from whom Jesus descended. Nevertheless, the three magi, shorn of their magical associations, redefined as wise kings from the Orient, became important figures in Christian iconography and legend.

Over the ensuing centuries definitions of magic were refined and new categories emerged as Christian, Islamic and Jewish theologians and scientists sought to understand better different aspects of magic rather than merely dismiss them. Magic was not one set of practices but an array that covered the spectrum of religious and scientific understanding. So in the medieval period the term 'natural magic' emerged as a means of differentiating between good and bad, or legitimate and illegitimate types of magic. Natural magic, or the wonders and secrets of God's world, was not the vanity of other cultures or religions but the key to unlocking the hidden properties of the material environment. Later, when the social scientists of the nineteenth century tried to make sense of magical practices in past and present cultures they too sought to categorise magic in terms of universal traits. This gave rise to the term 'sympathetic magic' to describe the occult or hidden relationships between things that had been in contact with each other or that shared superficial similarities. Magic could have a rational if false basis. But the power of magic as a rhetorical tool was ever dominant. The practice of magic continued to be defined in terms of the deceitful claims and strange practices of foreign magicians and priests.

Defining the other: magic as an accusation

So, across the centuries, religious groups have accused *others* of magic as a means of self-identification and to reinforce political and cultural legitimacy. In the context of early Christianity, this has been described in terms of magic as 'religious deviance'. The activities of early Christians – making the sign of the cross, the Eucharist, exorcism, speaking in tongues, nocturnal prayer meetings – smacked of magic to the Roman authorities. The accusation served to categorize Christians as antisocial outsiders inimical to Roman society and custom. In turn, the early Church Fathers developed a vocabulary that meant that magic was applied to the religions of a Rome portrayed as decadent and corrupt, and then became synonymous with all other religions except Christianity. More generally, monotheistic faiths have ever been ready to denounce polytheistic and animistic religions as being suffused with magic.

The three major Near Eastern monotheisms, Judaism, Christianity, and Islam, have also defamed each other in the same manner. The Christian Eucharist and worship of the Holy Trinity gave ammunition to Jewish and Islamic critics. Christians and Muslims have long persecuted Jews for supposed obscene magical rites, following in the footsteps of the Roman authorities in the Near East who considered them as magic-workers. In medieval Europe, the idea that the Jews practised obscene magical rights was deeply engrained in popular culture. In 1235, a pogrom took place in Fulda, Germany, after rumours circulated that Jews had ritually murdered Christian boys and used their blood in magical healing rites. The belief was widespread that Jews stole holy wafers from churches and pierced them until blood flowed which was then used in diabolic rituals.

Christians have also painted Islam as suffused with magic. According to the pioneering sociologist Max Weber, whose theories will be discussed in a later chapter, 'the propaganda of Islam in Africa rested primarily on a massive foundation of magic, by means of which it has continued to outbid other competing faiths despite the rejection of magic by earliest Islam'. Such claims came to the fore during the evangelical mission in Africa and the Middle East during the 19th century. So the American Calvinist missionary Samuel Marinus Zwemer, who began his evangelical mission in

Arabia in the 1890s, wrote that: 'In no monotheistic religion are magic and sorcery so firmly entrenched as they are in Islam.' I could provide ample evidence, however, to show that similar notions were equally entrenched in Christian America during the 1890s. A fundamental belief in the Old Testament edict 'Though shalt not suffer a witch to live' was widespread and occasionally acted upon. Folklore sources and court cases show that protective magic was practised across all ethnic and religious groups in the USA.

Magic has also been a means of delineating between true and corrupt forms of faith *within* religions. The early centuries of Christianity saw various sects, such as the Gnostics, denounced as adherents of magic. During the Reformation, the process of defining Protestantism involved identifying what were considered the magical elements of Catholicism. Various popes were denounced as necromancers, the miracles of the medieval saints were dismissed as magic, and priests and monks defined as peddlers of superstition defrauding a population cowed by fear. Relics and exorcisms were relegated from the sacred to the profane realm.

Within Islam, Sufism likewise attracted numerous accusations of magic. Sufism is often described as the mystical or esoteric dimension of Islam with its emphasis on ritual, asceticism, and attainment of individual spiritual enlightenment. The first *Tariqas*, or Sufi orders, were founded after the time of the prophet Muhammad. Sufi learning is based on oral transmission via masters whose spiritual influence can be tapped even after death, and whose tombs are therefore venerated. The 18th-century conservative Islamic reformer Muhammad Ibn Abd al-Wahhab (1703–91), and his followers, called for a purge of corrupting influences on Muslim devotion and the enforcement of a pure, 'original' form of Islam. The Wahhabi movement condemned the 'idolatry' of Sufi rituals, their worship of saints and mystics, and the veneration of tombs. In the early 19th century, under Wahhabi influence, tombs in and around the cities of Mecca and Medina were destroyed and Sufis were persecuted.

Some Islamic secularists, such as the founder of the modern Turkish state, Mustafa Kemal (1881–1938), also considered Sufism as a debased form of Islam that fostered magic and superstition, and kept people in a state of ignorance and credulity. The influential marabouts of North and West Africa, who are a cross between magicians and holy men, are considered an expression of Sufism, and so denounced as corrupting influences by orthodox Islamic reformers. They were equally denounced as charlatans by former colonial authorities too.

Similar reformist groups that aimed to root out magic can be found in other major religions. In late 19th-century India, the Hindu Swami Dayanand Saraswati (1824–83) launched a movement that preached a more monotheistic conception of Hinduism, as interpreted from his selective reading of the Vedas – the oldest Hindu scriptures. The sect he founded, *Arya Samaj*, continues to be active in parts of India today. Dayanand was inspired by the nationalist impulse to sweep away those aspects of Hinduism that had given ammunition to Christian and Islamic rulers who had painted it as a pagan, inchoate religion. Hinduism needed to be rationalized and aligned with the promotion of a scientific outlook. To achieve this, all forms of magical belief and practice had to be expunged. The Brahmin priesthood was identified as having corrupted the true faith of the Vedas, sowing magic, idolatry, and superstition. So magic as a retardant to progress and modernity, and yet also a barrier to restoring the purity of the past!

Magic as popular religion

When discussing the major religions of the world, the presence of magical beliefs and practices in people's everyday lives has often been considered by scholars as an aspect of 'little traditions', or of 'popular' or 'folk' religion. Such terms are, in themselves, problematic in that they can suggest a false impression of consensus, that people shared the same ideas and interpretations.

They can also suggest class or caste differences when the forms of religious worship concerned actually cut across social levels. But the terms can help to define general sets of beliefs and practices that are at variance with or condemned by official theology but which are not seen as irreligious or sinful by those who hold to them.

As we have just seen, religious reformers often considered magic as a deviant or corrupting form of religion, with specific religious groups often blamed as the source. Elements of popular religion were also identified by some authorities as the surviving remnants of religions that existed before the conversion of a population. We see this in Christian and Islamic history. In Europe, the early Church defined magic as pagan vestiges, and in the 19th century anthropologists developed the seductive notion that many of the magical practices of the European peasantry were survivals, cultural fossils, of prehistoric religions. Even such innocuous practices as the placing of a horseshoe above the door could be interpreted as an ancient *religious* practice.

As part of his campaign to enforce what he believed was a pure, 'original' form of Islam, Ibn Abd al-Wahhab categorized the belief in and practice of magic (*sihr*) as *shirk*, the Arabic term for idolatry and polytheism – equivalent to the Christian use of 'pagan'. He and other reformers were outraged that Muslims continued to consult magicians, worship the dead, trees, and rocks, seek the intercession of spirits, sacrifice animals, and profane sacred texts by using them as amulets and talismans. These 'un-Islamic' influences were attributed variously to the survival of ancient pre-Islamic practices, to converts who failed to divest themselves of their former beliefs and forms of worship, as well as to corrupting elements such as the Sufis. The Wahhabi movement would become a major influence on the formation of Saudi Arabia and contemporary Sunni Islamic fundamentalism. In Egypt, the liberal theologian and mufti Mohammed Abduh (1849–1905) also railed against the popular Islamic belief in magic. Even though the Koran seemed to

1. A Senegalise marabout at work

recognize the reality of magic, in his commentaries on the holy text Abduh denied there was any such thing: 'magic is either swindle or the result of the application of techniques unknown to the spectators'.

Yet as contemporary studies show, the magical practices of this 'popular Islam', as some scholars term it, remain central to the religious lives of populations such as the Arabian Bedouins, the urban populations of Egypt, and more generally to hundreds of millions of Muslims around the world. One example is the pilgrimage of Muslims in Kyrgyzstan to the shrines (*mazars*) of Solomon's Mountain, in the city of Osh. Here pilgrims seeking cures attach to sacred trees written invocations, requests for blessings, and colourful pieces of cloth. These practices have been interpreted as the continuation of pre-Islamic ancestor worship, but pilgrims do not see their activities as un-Islamic. The site's potent 'popular' religious history led to it becoming the country's first UNESCO World Heritage Site in 2009.

The practice of magic may be prohibited by Islamic authorities, but on the ground distinction is made between black and white magic (in Arabic, respectively *as-sihr al-aswad* and *as-sihr al-abyad*), between permitted and un-permitted uses of religion. As numerous Muslim informants in urban Malaysia told one researcher regarding black magic, 'we are not supposed to believe in it, but somehow it seems to work'. In popular religion, experience of magical misfortune and its magical cure trump the religious letter of the law, while authoritarian enforcement of the prohibition is generally moderated according to the purpose to which magic is put, and the motives behind the actions. Over the last few years, Amnesty International has been involved in several cases where the Saudia Arabian authorities handed out death sentences for black magic. In 2010, they highlighted the plight of a Sudanese national who had been paid to cast a spell on a man to make him leave his second wife and return to his first one. Three years earlier, the Saudi authorities had executed a pharmacist, an

Egyptian national, in part for similarly attempting to separate a married couple by magical means.

Another path to understanding the relationship between magic and popular religion is through the concept of syncretism, which basically means the blending or amalgamation of different religious traditions within a population. 'Syncretic' can be used in a pejorative sense, associated with 'primitive', 'illegitimate', 'artificial', or 'superficial'. The dominant religion might denounce the result of the process as magic or superstition. But used sensitively, it can also be applied to the way in which people appropriate and take control of theologies and cultural beliefs imposed upon them, adapting them to suit their own distinctive needs. In the context of magic, then, the continued resort to older religious practices is not a survival but an adaptation. The people using such practices consider them valid within their conception of what is acceptable to their faith.

Vodou is the obvious example of this syncretic relationship regarding interpretations of magic and religion. As developed amongst the people of Haiti, Vodou is a fusion of Catholic ritual and the religious beliefs and magical practices of the peoples of what is now Benin. Its development amongst the slave population of Haiti is inextricably linked with the fight for independence and emancipation during the late 18th and early 19th centuries. While essentially a monotheistic religion, Vodou worship incorporates a range of Catholic saints, African deities, and ancestor spirits. Vodou rituals involve elements that can be described in terms of magic or religion without either necessarily being taken as pejorative by its adherents.

Numerous other examples of similar syncretic belief systems have been identified, such as those born of the interplay between Islam and indigenous religions in West Africa. As one study observed, 'Islam in Africa is an African religion, obviously derived from outside but then adapted in many different ways to suit many different contexts.' Understanding the syncretic development of magical traditions also requires a consideration of the forces of globalization. A detailed study of the development of *brujería*, a blend of spiritualism, Catholicism, and diverse magical traditions in Puerto Rico, shows how the influence of Americanization, Caribbean immigration, and Asian products has shaped the demand and supply for the magical goods stocked by the popular religious supply shops known as *botánicas*. These have added new elements to practices forged from the island's Spanish Catholic and slavery past.

* * * *

The aim of this Introduction has been to show how magic is inextricably intertwined with the development of religion as a process of cultural negotiation. What looks like magic from the outside is understood, by those being studied or condemned, as the legitimate, practical application of religious worship – the everyday employment of religion for reasons other than spiritual enlightenment or salvation. As we now proceed through the tangle of interpretations, it will be useful to keep in mind these initial attempts at evaluating the meaning of magic. What the ensuing chapters will show, though, is that religion is only one part of the story of magic, for science is never far away.

Chapter 1
Anthropologies of magic

Evolutionary models underpinned early social scientific thought in the 19th century. In industrializing Enlightenment Europe, debate was focused on the historic place of religion in the development of society. In a series of lectures on the philosophy of religion published posthumously in 1832, the German philosopher G. W. F. Hegel (1770–1831) mapped out a novel pathway to understanding the global religious experience. Of significance was his ascription of equal importance to understanding how culture shaped the divine as to how religion shaped the mind. Hegel was not interested in magic *per se*, but he allocated a place for it in the first of the three stages of religion he devised. These three were: religions where nature was imbued with spirits; religions of elevated, individual, extra-terrestrial gods; and finally, Christianity, which he considered the 'consummate' synthesis of the other two. So magic was the 'oldest, rawest, crudest form of religion', which he identified as still existing amongst peoples such as the Eskimos.

The revolutionary political scientist Karl Marx (1818–83) may seem an unlikely figure to find in a study of magic. He did not reflect on the matter specifically, but his well-known views on religion are relevant to the discourse. They are encapsulated in his famous phrases, 'Man makes religion, religion does not make man', and of religion being the 'opium of the people'. Well versed in Hegelian thought but critical of it, the atheist Marx nevertheless agreed with the notion that the earliest form of religion concerned nature worship or what would later be termed 'animism'. Once again, this is where the origin of magic was rooted. At the other end of social development lay communism, by which point religion would have disappeared and there would certainly be no place for magic.

The theorizing of the first half of the century was concerned with 'stages' of development akin to the geological concept of stratification. The debate was transformed by the publication of Charles Darwin's *On the Origin of Species* in 1859. The language and model of biological evolution were now applied to social and cultural development. In the process, the category of magic came to assume more importance, and 'science' entered the scheme as the apotheosis of human development. That is not to say that definitions of magic were to become clearer; if anything, understanding of magic was to be muddied further.

The British polymath and social theorist Herbert Spencer (1820–1903) was the first to publish a social evolutionary model in which magic was conceived of as defining a proto-religion based on sympathetic associations and ancestor worship, but which, as a practice, was adaptable to the development of religion. Both could co-exist. But it was his rival Edward Burnett Tylor (1832–1917) who, as the first professor of anthropology at Oxford, caught the scholarly imagination and confirmed magic as a major topic in anthropological research. In his two-volume work *Primitive Culture* (1871), he set out a model whereby the human condition was universal but evolved at different rates. 'Savage thought', in his words, could and did exist in modern civilized society.

At the beginning, according to Tylor, there was magic as an expression of *animism* – the notion that things as well as humans have souls or spiritual essence. Animism and magic characterized peoples 'low in the scale of humanity'. Then religion as a distinct category developed from the concept of the human soul. The next evolutionary step was from polytheism to monotheism – a model that echoed Hegel's. Tylor coined the term 'survivals' for the elements of primitive culture that survived in the contemporary world, the study of which enabled the differential evolution of societies to be traced. In other words, it was not a matter of retrospective reconstruction. The evidence of the evolution process was all around in the customs of 'primitive tribes' and the European peasantry, just as Darwin found evidence for it in the animal world.

Tylor also coined the term 'pseudo-science' to describe magic. By this, he meant that, like science, magic explained and exploited the causal relationship between things. It was bad science, though, in that primitive assumptions and explanations about cause and effect were invariably wrong. Tylor's agenda was not merely that of the detached scholar, for he believed anthropology should have an explicit reformist agenda. While he was no advocate of organized religion, his invective was directed primarily against magic, which he described as a 'monstrous farrago', 'one of the most pernicious delusions that ever vexed mankind'. He likened primitive cultures to children, and like children they needed instruction if they were to develop to a higher stage of thinking.

Tylor's views were hugely influential, but it was the work of the Cambridge anthropologist James Frazer (1854–1941) that introduced the evolutionary model to the wider public. Avowedly inspired by Tylor's work, Frazer stamped his own mark upon the theory. In his thirteen-volume classic, *The Golden Bough* (1890–1915), he laid out a clear three-stage model of human intellectual development from magic, to religion, to science. All societies would eventually progress through these three stages. Frazer also made a more clear distinction between magic and religion than Tylor. Magic preceded religion, he argued. Religion, which he defined as 'a belief in powers higher than man and an attempt to propitiate or please them', was generally opposed to magic with its assumption of human control. Religion grew from a realization of the failure of magic. That said, he accepted that magical *practices* were not incompatible with religious *ideas*. Frazer also expanded on the comparison between magic and science. Magic was the 'bastard sister of science', based on two fallacious laws. One was the law of contagion, so that things that had been in contact with each other continued to have a relationship even at a distance. The other was the law of similarity – that like effects like. But if magic was ever proven to be true and efficacious, 'it would no longer be magic but science'.

The critics

The cultural evolutionary model may have been the bedrock of early anthropology, but the sheer weight of comparative material accumulated by Tylor and Frazer could not disguise the simplistic nature of the basic theory, and the definitions on which it rested were easily undermined. In an essay on 'Magic and Religion', Andrew Lang, a perceptive, belligerent critic of theories regarding the supernatural, rubbished Frazer's notion that religion evolved from the failure of magic. He did this by demolishing Frazer's interpretation of ethnographic reports regarding the supposed lack of religion amongst Australian aborigines.

A more influential critique flowed from the pen of the French sociologist Émile Durkheim (1858–1917). In his *Elementary Forms of the Religious Life* (1912) and other works, he rejected the idea that religion was defined exclusively in terms of gods and spirit entities, thereby undermining Tylor's and Frazer's definitions of magic at the same time. Instead, Durkheim saw religion as 'a unified system of beliefs and practices relative to sacred things'. He did not bother providing a clear definition of what he meant by 'sacred', though, other than 'the opposite of profane', thereby leaving plenty of scope for future debate. For Durkheim, religion was characterized by social integration and shared values and experience. Churches were an expression of a community. Magic, on the other hand, was concerned with transactions between individuals. As a mode of belief, it had no social binding function, and as a practice, it was concerned with servicing a clientele: 'There is no Church of Magic', declared Durkheim. Magic and religion shared similar beliefs, rites, and dogmas; it was their respective social function that divided them.

Whereas Durkheim addressed magic as an adjunct of his sociology of religion, his nephew Marcel Mauss (1872–1950) grappled with it head on. In his *A General Theory of Magic* (1902–3), Mauss took as a starting point his uncle's definition of magic as private and religion as collective. He then examined aspects of the sacred rituals practised by different societies and concluded that 'a magical rite is any rite which does not play a part in organized cults – it is private, secret, mysterious'. So far, so Durkheim, but Mauss did not see a fundamental breach between religion and magic. He had a self-stated preference for facts over theory. Magic and religious rites might be performed by different figures in many cultures, but they were often founded on the same conceptions. Some magic concerned the supplication of gods and religion. Rituals such as rain-making, for example, were performed in public open spaces. Religious texts and prayers could be used in magical contexts. Aspects of religion were based on sympathy in a Frazerian sense, but a lot of magic was not based on it or on contagion. Hence Mauss preferred to use the term 'magico-religious' in many instances. It has been widely adopted since, partly as a means of avoiding, often quite sensibly, the whole debate.

Mauss suggested that the religious impulse developed before magic. Religion was an expression of society, and magic developed as individuals appropriated the rituals and conceptions of the sacred for themselves. The German Jesuit and ethnologist Wilhelm Schmidt (1868–1954) came to a similar conclusion but from another intellectual direction. Turning the Spencerian and

Tylorian conception of evolution from animism to monotheism on its head, Schmidt proposed that the most primitive form of religion was in fact monotheistic. The primal worship of a supreme god, which he identified as still evident amongst the pygmies of Congo, degraded into magic, polytheism, and animism before entering a modern civilized form. Magic was therefore a degenerate form of religion. Schmidt's model nevertheless retained the sense that magic and monotheism did not operate on the same evolutionary level.

Another avenue of thought with its origins in these early debates, but which came to be fully defined theoretically decades later, is the idea that magic and religion can be best understood as symbolic constructions as well as cultural artefacts or intellectual stages. While influenced by Frazerian theory, the Franco-German folklorist Arnold van Gennep (1873–1957) fixed upon the symbolism of rites of passage across cultures and time as a gateway to exploring relationships between magic and religion. In his 1908 book *Rites of Passage*, he concluded that religion and magic co-existed, defining magic as ritual action, the techniques of religion. Looking deeper into the structure of a diverse array of rituals from around the world, he identified the importance of symbolic meaning in them. Ritual was built around 'life crises' or social thresholds, the transition from one social status to another. So the act of circumcision at puberty symbolized separation from the childhood state, for example. It was van Gennep who coined the now widely adopted term 'liminality' to describe these sacred thresholds in space and time, which symbolized spiritual as well as social boundaries, and the transition across them.

The symbolic approach of van Gennep and others, together with the psychological approaches discussed in the next chapter, encouraged scholars to explore the symbolic meaning of magic in terms of the body, its social representation, and the rituals associated with it. This in turn brought gender into the equation.

As Mary Douglas explored in *Purity and Danger* (1966), notions of bodily pollution are richly symbolic and are often gender specific. Orifices are boundaries with liminal social significance. They leak. They pollute. So numerous magical practices around the world are concerned with menstrual blood. Other excretions such as breast milk, saliva, and urine also have magical significance. Cleansing rituals are employed to restore bodily purity and harmonize social relations.

The symbolic interpretation also found expression in language. In 1930, parts of Frazer's *Golden Bough* were read to the Cambridge philosopher Ludwig Wittgenstein (1889–1951). The following year, he wrote down some remarks on Frazer's ideas. They only appeared in print in his posthumously published *Philosophical Investigations* (1953), though some preliminary remarks were omitted from the first edition. These began:

> I think now that the right thing would be to begin my book with remarks about metaphysics as a kind of magic. But in doing this I must neither speak in defence of magic nor ridicule it. What it is that is deep about magic would be kept.

As this suggests, Wittgenstein was critical of the notion that magic was false science, an early evolutionary stage. Magic interested him because it was an *expression*, a symbolic language. It 'gives a wish a representation; it expresses a wish'. On this basis, categories of modern and primitive thought break down.

The brief and cryptic nature of Wittgenstein's observations means that the meaning of his 'Remarks on Frazer's *Golden Bough*' are a matter of ongoing philosophical debate. In an anthropological context, the most incisive consideration of Wittgenstein's comments has been that of Stanley Tambiah (b. 1929). He starts from the basis that 'magical acts are ritual acts' and not applied science. His reading of linguistic philosophy then leads him to formulate magic not as bad science but as a rhetorical art. It is the combination of utterance and performance that, once enacted, engenders a change of state. Magic is done when the operator declares it will be done – at least if the performance has been conducted correctly. So when, in a Cornish charm for 'tetter' (ringworm), the charmer concludes his ritual treatment with the command 'Perish, thou tetter, and be though gone', magic has happened, an action has taken place: the words are not mere words.

Getting out of their armchairs

No scholarly discipline has grappled more with the concept of magic than anthropology. In fact, magic was the core of the new discipline and shaped its development. In the early days, it was preoccupied with exploring origins, but during the 20th century it began to focus more and more on the present. The discipline branched in different ways, mapping social, cultural, medical, and biological behaviour. The grand theories of magic and religion came under attack, or at least substantial modification, once anthropologists went out to test them by studying the 'primitive cultures' whose customs were referred to at second hand by Tylor and Frazer. In the process, the derogatory and racist aspects of cultural evolutionary theories were largely abandoned. It would no longer be taken for granted that magic was an aspect of the 'primitive', a survival antithetic to 'true' religion and science. The discipline also threw up new terms and phrases such as 'magical worldview' and 'limited good' to try and explain why magic *worked* for people.

When early anthropologists set off across the globe looking at the belief systems, social functions, and rituals of other cultures, they worked on the basis that the further from Western civilization geographically and technologically they could go, the more they would find out about human origins: the more exotic and remote the tribe, the more valuable the source material. They were testing the evolutionary model in the field.

The Polish-born British anthropologist Bronisław Malinowski (1884–1942) was a pioneer of such field anthropology. It was his fieldwork in the Pacific and Africa that formed the basis of the functional school of social anthropology that interpreted culture as having arisen to serve a social purpose. When the First World War broke out, Malinowski was in Australia engaged in an expedition to New Guinea. As a citizen of the Austro-Hungarian Empire, he faced internment, but he managed to pull some strings and found his way to the Trobriand Islands (Kiriwina Islands) off the eastern coast of Papua New Guinea. For the next few years, he immersed himself in the world of the fishermen and cultivators of this 'primitive' culture. Malinowski came to view the magical rituals they performed as sensible and understandable when experienced in their environmental and social context. Magic rituals provided emotional empowerment in the face of danger, and inspired solutions when alternative sources of knowledge (including science) were inadequate. In short, magic served a useful function. Independent of Wittgenstein, Malinowski also explored the role of language in magic, the meaning residing in the *use* of words. His attention turned to this whilst trying to translate the Trobrianders' magical formulae. The Islanders believed in the power of the words, but how to translate that quality? Prefiguring the work of Tambiah, he described how for the Islanders words were *actions* that achieved practical effects.

A curious thing happened when field anthropologists began to explore magical traditions in Africa. The preoccupation with 'magic', and all its baggage, receded as the categories of 'witchcraft' and 'sorcery' came to the fore. E. E. Evans-Pritchard (1902–73) was the key influence in this terminological shift. Influenced by Malinowski, Evans-Pritchard studied under the anthropologist A. R. Radcliffe-Brown (1881–1955), succeeding him as professor of anthropology at Oxford in 1946. Like Malinowski, Radcliffe-Brown had also headed to the opposite end of the globe in search of material. Between 1906 and 1912, he conducted pioneering trips to study the peoples of the Indian Ocean Andaman Islands

2. Bronisław Malinowski encountering a reputed Trobriander 'sorcerer'. From Malinowski's book *The Sexual Life of Savages in North-Western Melanesia* (London, 1929)

and the Australian aborigines. His approach was deeply influenced by the structuralism of Durkheim. Magic and religion should be understood as aspects of ritual, he thought. He had no truck with Malinowski's functionalist arguments. Magic could generate dysfunctional qualities such as fear and anxiety.

Evans-Pritchard followed a path between the two rivals. His work amongst the Zande people in Central Africa showed how beliefs that seemed irrational to Westerners were logical and sensible within the Azande's magico-religious conception of the world. Evans-Pritchard's influence on future anthropological terminology derived from the need to find what he felt were appropriately distinct English translations of Zande terms for different types of magical activity. So the Zande word *Mangu* was equated with 'witchcraft' in the sense of misfortune caused by people possessed of innate power (a physical substance in Zande conception) and inspired by envy or anger. *Ngua* broadly encapsulated magic and medicine in terms of ritual action. Evans-Pritchard then created

A BINSA SORCERER.

3. A 'sorcerer' from Binsa, now in the Democratic Republic of Congo. The American journalist Isaac Marcosson (1877–1961) related how a sorcerer from the Upper Congo region developed a reputation for his magical cures using a red substance that turned out to be tinned beef (*An African Adventure*, 1921). The magical foreignness of objects and substances was a widespread concept

'sorcery' as a distinct category of Zande *Ngua*. This he defined as the employment of magical techniques, medicines, or rituals to cause illegitimate harm to others. These clear definitions of witchcraft and sorcery, with magic as a general, less precise construct, came to dominate future anthropological discourse on African magic. But they are problematic. For one, the Evans-Pritchard definition of sorcery was different to that employed by those anthropologists, stretching back to Malinowski, who studied beliefs in Oceania. They used sorcery to described harmful magic generally and not just its morally illegitimate manifestations. So they included harmful magic to punish thieves, for example. More important, though, is that the focus on 'witchcraft' and 'sorcery' Evans-Pritchard inspired, and which was influenced by European definitions of witchcraft, led to a relative neglect of the broader, richer, but less familiar, complex worlds of African magic traditions.

Magical worldviews

In the early 1960s, dissatisfaction with the still pervasive 'old-school' theorizing of magic, religion, and science led Murray and Rosalie Wax to propose a seemingly fundamental shift in the study of magic. The Waxes, who had conducted fieldwork amongst the Oglala Sioux of the Pine Ridge Indian Reservation, South Dakota, criticized Frazerian and Durkheimian distinctions between magic and religion as based on Western Judaeo-Christian conceptions inappropriate for understanding other societies:

> The previous scholarly attempts to interpret magic had failed because in their concentration upon ritual, incantation, or wish-fulfilment, they had not truly understood how the persons in question conceived the world and the place within it of wish, spell, emotion, or ritual.

So studying the actions or symbols of magic was insufficient. They had to be interpreted within a conception of the world that was fundamentally different to the Western rationalist view. In fact, the Waxes suggested, the modern Western worldview was inimical to the 'magical worldview' ascribed to others. Lack of understanding led Western observers to describe as 'primitive', 'ignorant', or 'credulous' activities and beliefs that made perfect sense within the 'magical worldview'. Even when anthropologists developed a more sympathetic understanding (Malinowksi, for example), they still could not help rationalizing magical ideas in terms of Western definitions of scientific knowledge.

The term 'magical worldview' borrowed from the work of the Norwegian theological historian Sigmund Mowinckel (1884–1965). In his book *Religion und Kultus* (1953), Mowinckel had argued, on the basis of his Old Testament reading, that magic was not a form of religion but a 'worldview' – 'a particular way to understand things and their mutual connectedness'. That 'particular way', though, was based on conceptions of causal relationships, interconnectedness, that were fundamentally different to those developed in the modern West. The concept was also inspired by Robert Redfield's paper on 'The Primitive World View' published in 1952. Redfield (1897–1958) was a pioneer of 'worldview' theory, and saw it as a valuable means of comparing the ways of life of different societies. Anthropologists had spent too much time *looking in* upon societies, when they needed to understand how those societies *looked out* and made sense of the totality of the world around them.

Other anthropologists did not exactly greet the 'magical worldview' with wild enthusiasm. In a series of responses to articles written by the Waxes, the concept was pulled to bits. One criticism was that they were setting up a dichotomy as equally fallacious as those proposed by Durkheim and Frazer. Could all non-Western societies really be lumped together as sharing one magical worldview defined by its difference from the view born of Judaeo-Christian history? A major weakness was the Waxes' definition of the magical worldview in terms of the exchange of

Power, or *Mana* (the Pacific Islander concept of the spiritual force inherent in all things), between humans and nonhuman entities. Was this really the basis of all non-Western conceptions of the world? What of the European peasant? Did he hold both worldviews at the same time? One critic concluded that the Waxes' magical worldview was 'after all, nothing but Tylor's world of animism'. Other disciplines found value in the 'magical worldview', however, and the term continues to be quite widely used by historians, philosophers, folklorists, cultural theorists, and psychologists.

Another type of worldview was encapsulated in the theory of 'limited good' devised by the anthropologist George Foster (1913–2006) in the 1960s. It was inspired by his work on Mexican peasant societies, and attracted considerable debate in anthropological literature for a few years before dropping out of fashion. Foster identified a behavioural pattern of thought and action dictated by the perception that there is a limited good in the world. Society, economy, and natural environment constituted a closed system in which 'good', in terms of resources, was finite and static. So if someone got richer, it could only be at the expense of someone else. In a model 'classic' peasant society, people were locked into a moral economy which discouraged economic development. Wealth accumulation was abnormal, and countered by communal gossip and envy. The labourer asks him- or herself, 'I work just as hard as my neighbour, but he has become more prosperous. How can that be?' It was explicable in terms of the discovery of a resource, such as buried treasure, that was exceptional to the zero-sum economy. But it could also be explained in terms of magical appropriation.

Foster recognized the role of magic, witchcraft, and folk medical diagnoses in explaining misfortune in a limited good society. Other anthropologists, historians, and folklorists identified examples in the past and present from around the globe. Treasure legends from Peru to Sweden seemed to fit the model, with the possession of magical knowledge being one means of finding and securing treasure. Limited-good interpretations explained the basis of many witchcraft accusations, primarily as an explanation for misfortune. The Finnish concept of *onni* (luck, success) demonstrates this well. If a cow inexplicably stopped giving milk, then its owner's *onni* had decreased. In this case, another cow owner must have increased his or her *onni* through magic. This could lead to envy and result in accusations of witchcraft as a means of rebalancing the *onni*. Even if it did not get to this stage, the unfortunate cow owner would hope that another neighbour's cows would stop producing milk and the balance of *onni* would tip in his or her favour once again. The luck inherent in finding a good spouse was, likewise, governed by the increase and decrease of *onni* possessed by young women.

In some limited-good societies, envy also manifests itself in terms of the 'evil eye'. This is the notion that certain people can transmit misfortune or bad luck merely by looking at people or their property. The concept is not as pervasive as has sometimes been assumed. It is certainly a strong theme in Mediterranean and Near Eastern societies but less so in the annals of Western European witchcraft. While an attribute of witches, the ability to cast an evil eye was not necessarily restricted to those who held such a reputation. Those who cast an evil eye do so out of envy and jealousy. They do not benefit from it materially, but as a study of peasant communities in southern Italy explained, fear of the evil eye 'kept individuals and families from flaunting good fortune or material possessions directly', and so may have discouraged wealth generation.

As with all such embracing theories, limited good received a battering from some scholars as well as praise. But as Foster made clear, he did not claim it was applicable to all peasant societies, and noted that examples of 'limited-good' behaviour could be found in *all* societies. While it has gone out of fashion as a model of economic development (or the lack of it), it retains value as a conceptual tool for understanding some magical beliefs and practices across a wide range of cultures.

Worlds of magic closer to home

The folklorists of the late 19th and early 20th centuries were well aware of the continued belief in and practice of magic amongst European populations. They scoured the countryside recording Tylorian survivals. In doing so, they produced a valuable record for future social historians like myself. These supposed relicts of primitive thought were fitting for the amateur folklorist and antiquarian, but anthropologists rarely considered them worthy of serious anthropological investigation in the field. The inveterate European impulse to head overseas to explore magic cultures was weakened only from the 1950s onwards. A few anthropologists began to turn their gaze back to neighbouring societies, realizing that the 'traditional' belief in and practice of magic was not a subject restricted to the past or to overseas cultures.

In the early 1950s, after fieldwork in East Africa, the social anthropologist Julian Pitt-Rivers (1919–2001), a student of Evans-Pritchard, conducted a detailed study of life in an Andalusian village. The resulting book included a chapter on the 'supernatural' that concerned the role of *sabias*, or wise women. Magic was not the central concern of Richard and Eva Blum, either, when they conducted fieldwork on notions of health, life, and death in early 1960s rural Greece. But the Blums' anthropological approach demonstrated how engrained 'good magic', 'black magic', and 'sorcery' were in the religious and medical experiences of the Greek 'peasants' they studied. Illnesses were attributed to witchcraft, demons, nymphs, revenants, ghosts, and nature spirits. To combat these conditions, there were a variety of healers, wise women, and magicians. Like Mary Douglas, the Blums explored the centrality of pollution and purity to ritual healing. They also observed how priests were integral to this magical culture of protection and healing – religion and magic operating side by side.

In his book *Sud e magia* (1959), Ernesto De Martino (1908–65) applied anthropological, political, and psychoanalytic approaches to the meaning of magic amongst the rural poor of southern Italy, a region held by the northern Italian intelligentsia as a culturally distant and primitive place. His work attempted to rescue the culture of the south from such condescension. One of his key concepts for understanding magic was the 'crisis of presence'. There are critical moments in life, he explained, when people excluded from rational 'high culture' are confronted with an existential crisis over their non-existence, the loss of their souls, their erasure from history. Magic, as ritual, brought this condition to a head and enabled poor people to overcome these crises and so counteract feelings of depersonalization and alienation. In this sense, magic functioned as a psychological pressure valve.

The Mediterranean region, with its scattered, remote rural populations and belief in the evil eye, was an obvious destination for European anthropological fieldwork. It provided a fitting sense of distance from the Western urban industrial world. Today, Spain, southern Italy, and Greece remain a focus of research on folk medicine. The bigger step was exploring the prevalence of traditional magic in the rural lives of Central and Western Europeans – people living firmly in Frazer's age of science. Folklorists, educationalists, and clergymen were aware of the 'magical worldview' of Danish, German, Swiss, and French country folk in the post-Second World War era, but anthropologists were slow to take notice. When a few did, in the 1960s, they helped break down the old cultural and geographical divide between 'primitive' and 'modern' societies. Europeans were now treated to the same conceptual analysis as Pacific Islanders or African and South American tribes.

The French academic Jeanne Favret-Saada (b. 1934) was one of the first anthropologists to concentrate on the living tradition of magic in Europe – at least as understood in terms of witchcraft and unbewitching. In the late 1960s, she installed herself in a village in the Bocage (hedged country) of Lower Normandy, France, and became immersed in the intimate world of witchcraft accusations and exorcisms amongst the villagers. One finds some familiar anthropological themes in Favret-Saada's analysis. She considered witchcraft accusations and counter-magic as a symbolic discourse regarding the capture of individual power: 'witchcraft is spoken words; but these spoken words are power, and not knowledge or information'. Power she categorized as either a 'vital force' that everyone possessed (encompassing possessions, house, and land), or 'magical force', which was used by witches to capture 'vital force'. What was unusual was how Favret-Saada became part of the discourse, a victim of witchcraft and an agent in unbewitching, thus going beyond the anthropologist's usual role as neutral observer. In her subsequent analysis, though, she stepped back and adopted the academic position of making sense of her experience from an outsider anthropological framework.

Favret-Saada broke the mould, and numerous other French anthropology and sociology students headed for the French countryside during the 1970s and 1980s, comforted in the knowledge that home was just a few hours' drive away. Their findings have proved valuable for historians attempting to piece together the continued relevance of magic in post-Enlightenment Europe. Around the same time, the folklorist Inge Schöck revealed that magic was alive and well in southwest Germany, and the sociologist Hans Sebald argued that amongst the farming communities of Franconian Switzerland (a region in central Germany), where he had grown up, magic continued to serve an observable, functional purpose in regulating group conflict. He could see its function being eroded by social change, however, and the spread of 'scientific objectivity'.

Chapter 2
Historical perspectives

As the previous two chapters have already demonstrated, magic, as a belief and a practice, cannot be understood without an awareness of how its definition and operation have been shaped by history. But then we need also to be aware of how histories have been written. The early social scientists did not ignore the work of historians, but what they had to work with was religiously and culturally biased, generally based on limited sources, and equally puffed up with the sense of Western superiority. When historians began to delve deeply into the archives and detach themselves from the pervasive condescension towards the past, the theoretical divisions between religion, magic, and science formulated by the early social scientists broke down spectacularly.

Histories of magic

Where did magic come from? Long before anthropology came into existence, intellectuals had pondered the question. The answer was usually from the East, but how far east? The Roman naturalist Pliny the Elder (23–79 CE) provides us with the first concerted attempt to piece together the history of magic. According to Pliny's *Natural History*, there was 'universal consensus that magic began in Persia with Zoroaster'. Based on the calculations of the 4th-century BCE Greek mathematician Eudoxus, and the philosopher Aristotle, Pliny estimated that

Zoroaster lived 6,000 years before Plato, who was born in the 5th century BCE. Magic only reached the West, though, during the failed campaign of Persian King Xerxes against the Greeks. This took place in 480 BCE. A magician named Osthanes, whom Pliny believed was the first to write down magic, accompanied Xerxes and 'infected the world by the way at every stage of their travels'. And so, Pliny sighed, the Greeks developed a lust and madness for the magical art. He stated that Pythagoras, Plato, Empedocles, and Democritus had all headed East to learn more of the magic scattered by Osthanes and his fellow magi – whom he considered frauds and fools.

The works of Democritus (*c.* 460–370 BCE) were singled out as having been most influential in spreading the doctrine of Persian magic. Pliny's emphasis on Democritus, considered by some as the 'father of science', was due to Pliny's acceptance of the spurious attribution of magical and alchemical works to the man. One such text was the *Cheiromecta*, which explained the magical properties of plants, stones, and animals. Its real author was apparently a Greek-educated Egyptian named Bolus of Mendes. Pliny's history of magic also identified more recent branches of magic. One derived from 'Moses, Jannes, Lotapes, and the Jews, but living many thousand years after Zoroaster'. Another emerged in Cyprus.

Some early Christian authors followed the Greeks and Romans in ascribing the origin of magic to the human realm, mainly to Zoroaster and Osthanes, but several other names cropped up, such as two Egyptian magician-kings named Nectanebus and Bektanis. Fully incorporated into a Christian 'worldview', however, the history of magic required an Old Testament lineage and geography. The main narratives emerged in influential apocryphal literature, such as the *Pseudo-Clementines* ascribed to Bishop Clement of Rome, which circulated during the 4th century CE. According to the *Pseudo-Clementines*, fallen angels or demons taught magic to men. This echoed a Jewish tradition recorded in the Book of Watchers, part of the Book of Enoch, which possibly dates to the 3rd century BCE. According to this text, God's fallen angels, inspired by lascivious urges, rebelled and descended to earth to mate with mortal women, giving birth to giants. While on the loose, they taught their female consorts magic and herbalism.

The Christian emphasis was firmly on transmission of magic through the male line, though. According to the Pseudo-Clementine *Recognitions*, Ham, son of Noah, was the first to practise the newly acquired degenerate, demonic art. His knowledge survived the Great Flood, and passed down to Ham's son Mesraim and then to his descendants the Egyptians, Persians, and Babylonians. Mesraim was accordingly identified as Zoroaster (though, in other sources, Ham is Zoroaster). Epiphanius, a 4th-century Church Father, thought, however, that magic pre-dated Ham and fixed on Jared, who was a fifth-generation descendant of Adam. Nimrod is also a significant figure in these early histories of magic. Described in the Old Testament as the grandson of Ham, and associated with the great urban centres of Babel and Uruk, he accrued a mythical reputation as a great hunter and as rebellious in the face of God. According to Epiphanius, Nimrod founded the science of magic, and *Recognitions* tells how he received his knowledge of it in a flash of lightning from above. Nimrod too was considered by some early writers as one and the same as Zoroaster. Whatever the lineage, the Judaeo-Christian view was that magic was a product of the Babylonians, Persians, or Egyptians – from whom Moses learned a trick or two.

The New Testament introduced new characters to the story of the early transmission of magic. Simon Magus first appears in the New Testament Book of Acts, where he is described as a man from Samaria 'who had previously practised magic in the city'. We are told of his baptism and of his being admonished by Peter for offering money to obtain the secret of healing through the Holy Spirit by the laying on of hands. There is not much else to go on, and the transformation of Simon into the Magus, a great magician, and the father of all heresies, was created from texts written in the 2nd and 3rd centuries. One 4th-century manuscript, for instance, claims that Simon died after attempting to fly. The legend was further embellished and distorted over the next 18 centuries.

During the medieval period, the biblical Solomon, long a name to conjure with, came to the fore as the supposed source of magic or wisdom – depending on different contemporary points of view. Books of magic were formulated that purported to contain details of his rituals and conjuration to subjugate demons and achieve spiritual enlightenment. Hermes Trismegistus was another legendary figure of magic who had been in the picture for centuries, cited as the author of thousands of books on science and the occult or 'hidden' arts. A figure with multiple identities as a god and mortal, a syncretic mix of the Egyptian god Thoth and the Greek Hermes, Trismegistus became a major figure in the Renaissance magic tradition of the 15th century after a corpus of his supposed writings on occult philosophy was discovered and translated into Latin.

In a university lecture given in 1636, one Simon Ravensberg asked the rhetorical question: 'Can the first source of magic – i.e. where, when, etc. it first arose – be definitively demonstrated? No, it cannot.' Only one thing was certain, he continued, and that was that it was 'born along with idolatry, as though from the same egg'. It was, in short, the invention of demons. But such certainties were being questioned in the 16th and 17th centuries, as magic itself was defended or at least its history qualified.

In 1625, the French librarian and physician Gabriel Naudé (1600–53) wrote a book entitled *Apology for all the Wise Men Falsely Suspected of Magic*, which was translated into English in 1657 with the title *The History of Magick*. His aim was to rescue the reputations of the likes of Zoroaster, Socrates, Pythagoras, Virgil, and the medieval scientist Roger Bacon from centuries of false rumour and accusation. In the process, he gave a positive shine to magic itself. These great men of art and science, and others, had come under suspicion due to 'politicks, extraordinary Learning, Mathematicks, Suppositious Books, superstitious Observations, Heresy, Malice, Emulation, Ignorance, Credulity in Readers, and want of circumspection and Judgment in Writers'. Naudé distinguished between lawful and unlawful magic. Under lawful magic, he included divine or 'Mosoaicall Magick', in other words prophecies, miracles, and speaking in tongues. Then there was 'theurgic' magic, rendered operational by angelic communication. These types of magic exceeded human forces and originated from God. Natural magic, or the ability of the philosopher to understand occult properties, was also acceptable, and was first 'brought into vogue' by Zoroaster and Zamolxis, a Thracian man-god similar to the figure of Trismegistus. The only form of magic Naudé condemned was 'geotick' (goetic) or demonic magic, and 'men should not imagine any other Author of this perverse and unlawfull Magick than *Satan*'.

A similar position was adopted by the Welsh alchemist Thomas Vaughan (1621–66) in a pseudonymously published book entitled *Magia Adamica: or the Antiquitie of Magic* (1650). Vaughan disentangled the lineage of lawful and prohibited magic. 'Magic is nothing else but the Wisdom of the Creator revealed and planted in the Creature', he stated, and 'no word is efficacious in Magic, unless it be first animated with the word of God'. The world past and present continued to be full of false and devilish magicians, but the true magicians of antiquity were kings and prophets. So, following Vaughan, in the sense that God is the source of magic, there is no point at which it begins, only a point when it is divulged to humans. As the title of his book denotes, Vaughan, as others had suggested before him, believed that magic was revealed to Adam in Paradise before the Fall of man. 'Damnable and Devilish Magic' came after, and, as a good Protestant, Vaughan located one diabolic strand of it in the consecrations and exorcisms of the Roman Catholic Church.

During the 18th century, three further influences shaped understanding of the origin of magic. One was Freemasonry, an umbrella for a variety of secular and mystic fraternities. Interest in magical practice is certainly evident on the fringes of Freemasonry but the fascination with ancient symbolism was at its heart. The mystical aspect of Freemasonry centred on the architects of Solomon's temple and the mythology that developed around the story. This was given further resonance towards the end of the century by the growing interest in Egyptian antiquities. Jewish Kabbalah, or more precisely Renaissance Christian formulations of it, also fed into the interest in the rituals and symbols that might unlock ancient wisdom. So in some educated quarters, Freemasonry gave a new impetus to exploring the history of magic.

Another 18th-century development took the story of magic in a new compass direction. On the back of the success of the East India Company, and the consolidation of British rule over the continent, European interest in the culture and history of India flourished. This was encouraged by Warren Hastings (1732–1818), the first governor-general of India. Scholars set about translating ancient Indian Sanskrit texts into English for the first time, thereby opening up a new world of ancient religious and magical knowledge for an educated public back home. German and French philologists and Orientalist scholars followed suit.

Also during the late 18th century, what appeared to be a sensational scientific breakthrough promised an answer to the origin of magic as an *effect*. The Viennese doctor Franz Anton Mesmer (1734–1815) postulated that an invisible magnetic fluid existed inside the human body that could be channelled to influence other bodies. He and his followers used this 'animal magnetism' to heal the sick by unblocking the channels of flow either through will power or physical contact. The basic concept was adapted and developed in different ways by others. Hypnotism has its scientific origin in animal magnetism, for

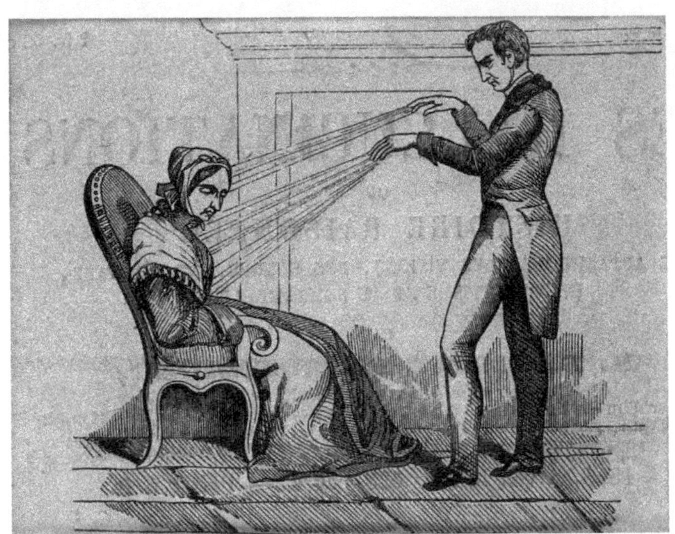

4. A mesmerist directs his animal magnetic forces towards a woman, who responds with convulsions

example. In Germany, students of animal magnetism had a strong mystical streak. The proposed universal nature of this magnetic fluid explained the trance states of religious ecstasy, communications with the spirit world, and some of the non-fraudulent powers attributed to magicians in history.

The physiology professor Joseph Ennemoser (1787–1854) was one of these German investigators, influenced by all the developments just outlined. His book *Geschichte des thierischen Magnetismus* (1844) was published in English in 1854 under the title of *The History of Magic*. The two-volume work was translated by the spiritualist William Howitt and his son during a voyage to Australia in 1852 – 'when American spiritualism was little heard of in England, and undreamed of by us'. While surveying the classical and Renaissance literature on the history of magic, Ennemoser was led to a novel conclusion by his knowledge of

Asian religion and myth. He surmised that the origin of magic lay not in Persia, Egypt, or amongst the Jews, but lay even further East. Magic, in its 'true and original meaning' as a communion with the world of spirits, the study of nature, and as 'a peculiar and inborn gift of the human soul', originated in Asia.

Ennemoser's evidence derived from the translations of ancient Indian Sanskrit religious texts such as the Law Code of Manu, which dates back some two thousand years or more, the Vedas, as well as other related sacred tomes such as the Zoroastrian *Zendavesta*, and Chinese texts. According to Ennemoser, by the time of Zoroaster, magic had already become corrupted and misused, divided into black and white qualities. He suggested that 'the later teachings of the magicians of Egypt, of Alexandria, and the middle ages, were founded on the views of the Oriental, Jewish, and Greek antiquity, and only changed and varied to suit the age'. The periodical *Westminster Review* dismissed Ennemoser's book in withering terms:

> We feel that we are stretching a point in affording a place even in the outskirts of science to Ennemoser's 'History of magic'. Such a subject, adequately handled by a competent and scientific thinker, might furnish a fertile theme for comment; but it can only be a matter of regret that Dr Ennemoser's innocent, but very moon-struck speculations have not been allowed to rest in the obscurity of their primitive tongue.

Many, however, found it a source of great inspiration and erudition. It went on to be widely referenced by psychologists, historians, anthropologists, and occultists, and piqued the interest of such literary figures as Dickens and Gaskell.

While Ennemoser's *History* achieved wide cultural recognition, another influential 19th-century 'history of magic', by the French mage Alphonse Louis Constant (1810–75), better known as Éliphas Lévi, became one of the foundation stones of modern occultism. In his 1860 *Histoire de la Magic*, Lévi reiterated a familiar classical and biblical lineage for magic, albeit with a few tweaks. Magic was the 'transcendental science, the absolute science' of Abraham, Confucius, and Zoroaster, graven on stone by Enoch and Hermes Trismegistus. But Lévi could not ignore the now accessible ancient Sanskrit magico-religious texts. Believing that India had been founded by the descendants of the banished biblical Cain, Lévi saw it is the home of black magic, 'goetia', and pernicious workers of illusion. India was the mother of all idolatries, the origin of false magic characterized by 'a thousand deformities, which terrifies reasonable minds and provokes the anathemas of all the understanding churches'.

Inspired by Kabbalah and his own Catholicism, Lévi represents one major branch of modern occultism that located magical enlightenment as a Western Judaeo-Christian tradition. Another branch looked to the East. Its most influential proponent was the Theosophical movement founded by the medium Helena Petrovna Blavatsky (1831–91). Having travelled the globe seeking spiritual knowledge, and picked her way through various mystical traditions, Blavatsky identified the source of all ancient wisdom as residing in India and Tibet. It was personified by the mysterious mahatmas, or holy men, mortals who had transcended to a higher spiritual state, from whom she claimed to derive spiritual powers. She believed India was the cradle of the Egyptian race. It is no surprise to find that Blavatsky relied heavily on the English translation of Ennemoser for her understanding of the history of magic, and it no doubt shaped her conception of secret knowledge spreading from East to West. One of her early followers, the British-born American medium Emma Hardinge Britten (1823–99), edited a book entitled *Art Magic: Or Mundane, Sub Mundane, and Super Mundane Spiritism*, in which the case for looking even further East was also made: 'Few nations of the East exhibit a greater amount of devotion to magic than the Chinese, a people whose antiquity is the problem of history, whose priority of origin disputes the palm even with India.'

Published histories of magic are nearly all concerned with the ancient world and Europe, but many other cultures around the globe have their histories too, though little has been written about them. In many societies, they are expressed orally through myth and legend. The Trobriand Islanders studied by Malinowski had two mythic explanations. One was that magic was first brought to light by the ancestor spirits that dwelled in an underground realm from which all life emerged. Another myth explains how magic was first given to people by the heroic figure of Tudava, who created some of the islands by throwing stones into the sea, and from whom people were given the gift of cultivation. An early study of the Kalahari Bushmen by the amateur anthropologist Louis Fourie recorded that they believed that magic derived from an evil spirit called the *gaua*, who received the spirits of those who had died a 'bad death'. Fourie equated the *gaua* with Satan, which again raises the issue of being aware that the impulse to find analogies in Western Christian history might distort or misrepresent the beliefs of other cultures.

Between heresy and science

Various forms of magic, *mageia*, had a dirty reputation in late Greco-Roman society, and were often referenced under the ill-defined heading of *superstitio*. This was magic defined as consisting of alien rituals, usually harmful in intent, linked with poisoning, and practised for filthy lucre. Magic was not distinct from religion but rather an unwelcome, improper expression of it – the religion of the other as described in the first chapter. As the Christian Church set about the task of converting the known world, it appropriated the language and definitions of antiquity in order to define exactly what was good and bad religion. In the process, the clearest lines yet were drawn between religion and magic in the historical record.

The Church was categorical in its equation of magic with paganism – in other words, all religions other than Judaism and

Christianity. Magic was redefined by the likes of St Augustine of Hippo (354–430) as explicitly demonic. The gods and spirits worshipped by non-Christians past and present were, therefore, nothing more than demons and devils. In this sense, the origin of magic lay in Hell. Humans could not perform magic without demons, and even then its effects were nothing more than the slippery illusions and pretences that defined superstition. It was the Christian mission to expunge magic from the world, but magic *per se* did not pose a fundamental threat. This situation changed from around the 12th century.

One reason for the intellectual interest in magic in medieval Christian Europe was the flourishing scientific and mystical scholarship of Muslims and Jews in Spain and southeastern Europe. Islamic and Jewish cultures had preserved antique philosophical and medical texts lost to Europe, and had developed their own innovative theories on the workings of the world. In one of those all too rare episodes of collaborative exploration, Christian, Islamic, and Jewish scholars shared their combined wisdom. The common magic of the people was mere superstitious trash, but the literary archive of magic might contain revelatory knowledge about the occult or hidden forces that shaped existence. The quest was to separate out the natural from the demonic, the sacred from the profane, the beneficial from the harmful, and to identify magic that worked and why. In the realm of *natural* magic, alchemy and astrology were identified as worthy of particular investigation. This enquiry extended to medicine through investigation into the occult or hidden power of plants, animals, and gem stones.

The views of the famed 13th-century scientist and theologian Roger Bacon demonstrate the difficulties the medieval scholars faced in separating magic from science and religion. Bacon saw science as a weapon against the falsity and 'nullity' of magic, but ultimately could not draw a complete line between them. He accepted that certain herbs, stones, and metals possessed 'almost miraculous' powers, some verbal incantations might work through the power of thought and soul, the stars could influence the minds and bodies of people. In short, without explicitly stating as much, he accepted natural magic worked as an occult science.

The American historian Lynn Thorndike (1882–1965) pioneered the reappraisal of medieval magic. As he wrote in the first of the eight volumes that made up his *History of Magic and Experimental Science*:

> My idea is that magic and experimental science have been connected in their development; that magicians were perhaps the first to experiment; and that the history of both magic and experimental science can be better understood by studying them together.

While he recognized that this relationship stretched back into ancient civilizations, his focus was very much on the 12th and 13th centuries as a formative period in the development of modern science. Although influenced by the early anthropologists, what Thorndike demonstrated helped undermine the Frazerian evolutionary model by showing how, as personified by the medieval and Renaissance scholar, magic, religion, and science were entwined in intellectual development. Or, as another leading historian of medieval magic, Richard Kieckhefer, put it, 'magic is a crossing-point where religion converges with science'.

One of the outcomes of this medieval and Renaissance era of occult exploration was an increase in the power that theologians ascribed to demons. This, in turn, fed growing fears over the Satanic threat to Christianity. If natural magic was occult science, demonic magic was heresy. Magic was no longer an expression of paganism but instead the perversion of Christianity. The Church began to investigate the activities of real and supposed practitioners of demonic magic, or necromancers as they were frequently called. This was the magic of conjurations and adjurations based on Christian ritual, which circulated amongst the learned elites in Europe's monasteries and universities via books or grimoires. The more magicians the Church unmasked, and the more grimoires its inquisitors found and burned, the more it became clear to them that demonic magic, and perhaps all magic, was a part of a growing Satanic conspiracy. During the 15th and early 16th centuries, the concern over the diabolic nature of learned magic spread to encompass the 'superstitions' of the general populace, giving rise to the era of the witch trials of the 16th and 17th centuries.

The laws against witchcraft instituted across Europe in the first half of the 1500s were also laws against magic more generally – a fact that often gets lost due to the historians' preoccupation with the witch trials. An English Statute of 1542 laid out penalties for a range of magical activities including treasure seeking and theft detection, while the Scottish Statute of 1563 prohibited 'using witchcraftis, sorsarie and necromancie'. In Scotland, the threat of execution hung over all who practised magic. Laws elsewhere, such as the Holy Roman Empire's Carolina Code of 1532, and a Danish statute of 1617, set out milder punishments for 'beneficent' magic – in other words, magic misguidedly deemed good by the general populace but to be suppressed as implicitly Satanic. Yet while secular and ecclesiastical authority drove a wedge between magic and religion, engaged in a campaign to exterminate the former to save the latter, there were some, like Thomas Vaughan, who continued to make the case for the sacred role of magic.

Neither did the scientific community concertedly distance itself from the parameters of magic, despite its demonization by theologians. Occult philosophies founded on Neoplatonism, a conception of the world developed in late Roman antiquity that espoused the spiritual interconnectedness of everything, continued to be a powerful intellectual force. This was in part because magic continued to offer novel avenues of experimental investigation, and partly because to deny the belief in magic, or at least its diabolic expression, was to attract accusations of atheism. The contribution of magic to the 'scientific revolution' of the 17th century has been a matter of considerable debate. While one camp of historians sees the scientific revolution as a consequence of the rejection of magic, others have argued that magical experimentation was integral to the eventual generation of new, non-magical scientific principles. The latter trace connecting threads of intellectual endeavour from Renaissance magicians who re-examined the wisdom bequeathed from antiquity, such as the Neoplatonist networker Marsilio Ficino (1433–99) and the German occult philosopher Cornelius Agrippa (1486–1535), through the writings of such 16th-century influences as the mathematician and astronomer Giordano Bruno (1548–1600), who was burned at the stake, and the activities of the Elizabethan mage John Dee (1527–1608), and finally to the giants of modern science like Isaac Newton (1642–1727). The pursuance of natural magic, alchemy in particular, to which Newton devoted considerable time, inspired the empirical investigation of the world that generated theoretical leaps into a new age of science.

At a popular level, scientific knowledge continued to be equated with magical ability. This was most clearly expressed with regard to mathematics. Indeed, the mathematician John Wilkins (1614–72), founding member of the Royal Society, entitled his book on the 'mechanical arts' *Mathematicall Magick*, 'in allusion to vulgar opinion, which doth commonly attribute all such strange operations unto the power of Magick'.

The triumphalist histories of witchcraft written in the 19th and early 20th centuries, which depicted the witch trials as a product of an irrational, unscientific medieval mind, and the end of the witch trials as a product of a modern scientific revolution, were misguided in their understanding of the period and naive in their espousal of evolutionary models of progress. As historian Stuart Clark has suggested, the demonological theories that bolstered the witch persecution enjoyed a scientific as well as a theological status. It is, furthermore, difficult to find direct causal links between developments in scientific materialism and popular or judicial scepticism. True, by the 18th century, magic was largely uncoupled from scientific endeavour, but the development of science did not exorcise magic. Scepticism regarding magic did not depend on science providing satisfactory answers for the workings of the world. As a consequence, magic as a practice, as an idea, and as a creative force, was by no means banished from modern Western society.

Disenchantment?

In a 1917 lecture, the German sociologist Max Weber (1864–1920) coined the term '*Entzauberung der Welt*' – the 'disenchantment' or 'demagification' of the world. The latter word is awkward but it is a more accurate translation of *Entzauberung*. Yet 'disenchantment' has become the literary norm in scholarly discourse, so I shall stick with it. *Entzauberung* encapsulated Weber's history of the transition to modernity through the elimination of magic from religion. For Weber, magic was an impotent art; it promised to give humans control over a natural world governed by spirits, but was ever destined to fail. He sketched out distinctions between religion and magic but was well aware that they were neither hard and fast, nor necessarily fitted the historical evidence. He thought the earliest forms of religion were essentially magical, and that aspects of 'magical religion' survived through subsequent stages of human thought – as was evident in Roman Catholicism. So far, so familiar. After all, Weber was influenced by the anthropological and sociological theories described in the previous chapter. Weber's ideas are introduced here because of his view that 'only ascetic Protestantism completely eliminated magic'.

In his *Protestant Ethic and the Spirit of Capitalism* (1904), published years before he came up with the encapsulating term *Entzauberung*, Weber postulated that Protestantism was a watershed in the development of modern Western society. Its disenchanting effect on both individual psychology and social organization promoted scientific rationalism and a capitalist ethic. As he later explained, a disenchanted world 'means that one can, in principle, master all things by calculation . . . One need no longer have recourse to magical means.' It did not mean the end of religion, the denial of a divine principal, but rather an ambiguous freedom from the bondage of a life preoccupied with maintaining relations with supernatural forces.

Weber's notion that the Reformation liberated religion from magic, and inspired 'technical rationality', had a considerable influence on the way in which historians interpreted the rise of science, the expansion of commerce, and the path to the Enlightenment in the early modern period. The title and central argument of Keith Thomas's classic study *Religion and the Decline of Magic* (1971), which covers English history from the medieval period to the 18th century, echo Weber's 'Disenchantment of the World'. Thomas recognized, though, that the Reformation also promoted concerns about magic that were actually only assuaged a couple of centuries later during the Enlightenment. In this respect, Protestantism was a fundamental but *transitional* stage on the way to a modern rational society in England.

Over the last 20 years or so, historians have increasingly chipped away at the disenchantment thesis, exposing its deeply problematic foundations, and partly undermining Thomas's thesis in the process as well. First, elements of disenchantment can be found prior to the Reformation. Second, the failures of the Reformation are now highlighted as much as the successes thanks, in part, to detailed archival work on church court records. It is now clear that Protestant authorities struggled to make people think like good Protestants and to suppress private adherence to Catholic ritual activity. Some historians now talk of a 'long Reformation' to characterize this. Furthermore, Protestantism may have espoused a rational and enlightened religion, but while it attempted to sweep away the magical religion of Catholicism, its tenets also reinforced and promoted certain aspects of magic. So, for example, the emphasis on the possession of the Bible, and the promotion of access to it, facilitated the widespread magical use of the Bible in popular cultures – as we shall see in a later chapter. Historians are also now much more aware of the continuance of 'magical worldviews' in modern industrial societies across the globe, at all social levels, and less likely to uncritically accept the old evolutionary notions of social and intellectual progress.

Chapter 3
All in the mind?

In recorded history, there have always been sceptics regarding the reality of magic, and those who railed at the empty boasts of magicians. A seminal treatise entitled *On the Sacred Disease*, attributed to the 5th-century BCE physician Hippocrates, denounced magicians, the divine cause of diseases they espoused, and the rituals they employed. He focused on epilepsy in particular, a condition that was popularly considered a sacred affliction, and which therefore provided a convenient get-out clause for those who claimed to wrestle with the supernatural. The butts of his withering critique were:

> Magicians (*magoi*), purifiers (*kathartai*), beggar-priests (*agurtai*) and charlatans (*alazones*); the very same who pretend that they are particularly pious and know much. Accordingly these individuals, by hiding behind divinity and setting it forth as a pretext for their helplessness, make use of it so that, not knowing anything, they are not exposed.

Hippocrates was no sceptic regarding divine intervention, but he objected to the notion that divinities corrupted human bodies. The gods were in the business of purifying not polluting mortals. We find similar sentiments expressed in satires such as those of Lucian of Samosata, who lived in the 2nd century CE. Lucian repeatedly played on the folly of superstition, and derided those who 'purge themselves with sacred medicine, others are mocked by chants impostors sell, and other fools fall for the spells of Jews'. A pattern begins to emerge here though: unmask the magician but refrain from saying explicitly that magic does not exist. This Hippocratic attack on *practitioners* was a template for scepticism that was followed pretty much up to the Enlightenment.

One of the most fascinating ancient perspectives relevant to scepticism regarding magic is found in the philosophy of the radical Greek thinker Epicurus (341–270 BCE). He relegated the gods to such a distance from the lives of men that the prayers and adjurations of mortals could but only fail to attract divine attention. Believe only what you have observed or deduced, he taught. His deductions included that the world was governed by colliding atoms and not spirits. There was no divine inspiration or guiding hand over the world of humans. Unfortunately, only fragments of his writings have come down to us, but from what we know of his ideas, there was little room for magic.

Expressions of scepticism or doubt regarding the reality of magic during the medieval period were concerned with specific types of magic rather than its wholesale dismissal. Magic was too entwined with theology and experimental science. During the 16th century, though, the Reformation and the impact of the witch trials generated a small but significant number of educated people who expressed concerns about the rationality of magical belief. These debates even extended to suggesting that the age of miracles had long since ceased. One consequence was greater attention to providing explanations for what caused the seemingly magical. Two areas of debate came to the fore: magic as deception and illusion, and magic as a psychological condition.

Just an illusion?

Illusion had long been recognized as a component of magic in its broader sense. The 14th-century Arabic scholar Ibn Khaldūn described the 'magic' of prestidigitation (*sh´wadha*) as the exercise of influence upon the powers of the imagination. The practitioner planted among his audience 'different sorts of phantasms, images, and pictures... Then, he brings them down to the level of sensual perception.' In reality, though, nothing they produced existed in the external world. There were also physical illusions, of course. The 10th-century Baghdad scholar al-Bāqillānī provided the example of the deception of filling a silk bag with mercury to make people think it was a slithering snake. But there was a supernatural interpretation too, which brought illusion into the sphere of illicit magic. The Devil was portrayed as the greatest illusionist of all, and his disciples, the magicians and witches, could call upon his power in this respect. There was considerable debate about what illusions the 'Witch of Endor' had used to fool King Saul into thinking she had conjured up the spirit of the prophet Samuel to divine his future. This was an act of necromancy in ancient Greek terms, but in Christian theology arguments raged over the reality or otherwise of this episode, as recorded in the Old Testament Book of Samuel.

Two English sceptics, the Elizabethan gentleman Reginald Scot (*c.* 1538–99) and the mid-17th-century author Thomas Ady, stuck their necks out because of their concerns over the misery the witch trials were causing in their communities. Scot was the more outspoken of the two in terms of his rejection of the possibility of demonic magic, relations with spirits, and miracles. But both placed considerable emphasis on the art of juggling, or what we would call stage magic today. By explaining how tricks were performed, they hoped to demonstrate that many of the manifestations attributed to magic or witchcraft could easily be replicated by props and sleight of hand. Scot set himself the not inconsiderable task of learning the tricks of the trade, as performed by the numerous itinerant illusionists who plied their trade at markets and fairs. He felt a pang of remorse in publishing his exposé 'to the hinderance of such poore men as live thereby'. But he heaped scorn and abuse upon the other main group of

5. Depiction of a medieval juggler, from an 11th-century French manuscript

tricksters in his view – the Catholic clergy. Protestant writers loved to illustrate how the priesthood used illusions to make people believe the efficacy of their exorcisms, or made them think they were in the presence of the spirits of the dead in order to bolster the belief in the money-making concept of purgatory.

Amongst the many tricks explained in Scot's book, *The Discoverie of Witchcraft* (1584), we find how to convey 'one or manie balles into nothing', 'to conveie monie out of one of your hands into the other', 'to cut a lace asunder in the middest, and to make it whole againe', 'To eate a knife, and to fetch it out of anie other place', and, most impressive of all, 'To cut off ones head, and to laie it in a platter'. Ady sought to show how such trickery had direct analogies with the phenomena witnesses were attributing to witches in court. He was writing a few years after the witch hunt instigated in eastern England by the Witchfinder General, Mathew Hopkins (d. 1647). Claims that witches possessed devilish imps or familiars in the guise of domestic animals appeared over and over again in the evidence against the hundreds of suspects who were rounded up. So Ady suggested how these familiars could be reproduced by the juggling arts. The juggler possessed,

> the skin of a Mouse stopped with feathers, or some like Artificial thing, and in the hinder part thereof sticketh a small springing Wire of about a foot long, or longer, and when he begins to act his part in a Fayr, or a Market before Vulgar people, he bringeth forth his Impe, and maketh it spring from him once or twice upon the Table.

As to the techniques of distraction that accompanied these tricks, Thomas Ady recalled

> one man more excelling in that craft than others, that went about in King *James* his time, and long since, who called himself, *The Kings Majesties most excellent Hocus Pocus*, and so was he called, because that at the playing of every Trick, he used to say, *Hocus pocus, tontus talontus, vade celeriter jubeo*, a dark composure of words, to blinde the eyes of the beholders, to make his Trick pass the more currantly without discovery, because when the eye and the ear of the beholder are both earnestly busied, the Trick is not so easily discovered, nor the Imposture discerned.

Words – the 'hocus pocus' of magic – carried no power, but were merely diversionary. As Scot explained, 'words of art' were used 'partlie to protract the time, and partlie to gaine credit and admiration'. Such 'Juggling Tricks' explained away the reputation of Simon Magus, and the dubious miracles of the pagan priests of the ancient world. In short, they debunked biblical magic, cleansing the Holy Book of 'superstitious' interpretations.

Ventriloquism, or belly-speaking, was another art that could seem magical. One 17th-century glossary defined 'ventriloquist' as 'one that has an evil spirit speaking in his belly; or one that by use and practice can speake as it were out of his belly, not moving his lips'. The Dutch witchcraft sceptic and physician Johann Weyer (1515–88), an admirer of *On the Sacred Disease*, reflected on how belly-speaking had been used to deceive and exploit the credulous. He reported cases where voices emanated from under armpits and from women's vaginas. An Italian reported a case of the latter from the town of Rovigo.

> He repeatedly heard the voice of an unclean spirit – quite faint, to be sure, but perfectly intelligible, and amazingly accurate on the subject of things past or present, but generally uncertain about the future, and often idle and fallacious.

Ventriloquism was frequently put forward as an explanation for the deceptions performed by the Witch of Endor, Greek oracles, and Catholic priests who fabricated ghosts. It was also thought to explain some cases of supposed demonic possession.

'Busying the senses of hearing and seeing', as Thomas Ady put it, was the key to the imposture of magic. Incantations and ventriloquism deceived the ears, and sleight of hand could make things appear and disappear. The organ of sight could also be manipulated by technological forms of artifice. *Magia optica*, a branch of natural magic, was performed by the use of lenses, prisms, and mirrors to generate external images that fooled the eyes. There are 'divers ways to see, that one thing may seem to be another', observed the Neapolitan occult scientist Giambattista della Porta, who devoted considerable inquisitive energy to exploring this topic. In his much reprinted and hugely influential work *Magiae naturalis* (1558), there were instructions on how 'To see in a Chamber things that are not', and how to create 'An Image to be seen by a hollow Glass'. Here are his instructions to make an image fly in the air:

> If any man would do it, it is easily done thus: Fit two pieces of wood together like a square or gnomon of a Dial, and being well fastned, they may make an Angle as of a right angled triangle, or Isosceles. Fasten then at each foot one great Looking-glass, equally distant, right one against the other, and equidistant from the Angle: let one of them lye flat, and let the spectator place himself about the middle of it, being somewhat raised above the ground, that he may the more easily see the form of the heel going and coming: for presently you shall perceive, if you set your self in a right line, that cuts that Angle, and it be equidistant to the horizon. So the representing Glass will send that Image to the other, which the spectator looks into, and it will shake and move the hands and feet, as Birds do when they fly. So shall he see his own Image flying in the other, that it will always move, so he depart not from the place of reflection, for that would spoil it.

Della Porta also played around with the camera obscura, from which modern photography originated. It consisted of a box fitted with a convex lens, into which bright natural light was admitted. The light was projected onto a white surface in a darkened room. To someone placed in the darkened room who did not know what objects were present in the lit room, the effect was 'magical' – even if the images were upside down. By using an additional mirror, della Porta was able to turn the projection the right way up, to stunning effect. In the 17th century, developments in lens technology, the placement of a light source in the box, and the production of glass slides, led to the creation of the aptly named 'magic lantern'. Projecting images of skeletons and devils painted on slides were popular and sensational. As was observed in the

1670s, persons of great courage had 'chang'd pale at the sight of these Sports and of these Magical Artifices'. By the 18th century, magic lantern shows were touring the provinces, and some of their operators were clearly not averse to presenting their projections as 'real' magic.

Magic against magic

Although jugglers and fairground conjurers were often considered as fraudsters playing upon the credulity of the poor, and as pests by officials preoccupied with vagrancy and petty crime, they also served a positive social function. In Thomas Ady's words, they could act as 'a candle in the dark', their public demonstrations doing more to debunk 'superstition' than denunciations from the pulpit or the frustrated writings of the sceptical. As Scot explained, the doings of jugglers 'are not onlie tolerable, but greatlie commendable'. They 'alwaies acknowledge wherein the art consisteth, so as thereby the other unlawfull and impious arts may be by them the rather detected and betrayed'. But the self-appointed role of illusionists as enlightenment agents only began to be adopted seriously from the late 18th century onwards.

In their advertisements, puffs, and performances, ventriloquists and illusionists espoused their public role as educators. Some adopted the title of 'professor', while others described themselves as philosophers and mathematicians. They were purveyors of 'rational' recreation. The Scottish magician and ventriloquist John Rannie, who became a sensation in America during a tour in 1801, advertised his desire 'to open the eyes of those who still foster absurd belief in GHOSTS, WITCHES CONJURATIONS, DEMONIACS, &c.' Stage magic also became an 'infotainment' staple of the halls of public science that were instituted as commercial ventures during the early 19th century. In England, the most famous of them all, the Royal Polytechnic Institution, put on demonstrations of the science of magical trickery, along with its exhibitions of electricity, engines, magic lanterns, chemical reactions, and optics. From the 1850s onwards, the 'magic' of spiritualist mediumship provided its lecturers with plenty of extra material.

The crusading magician also served a political colonial role as well. British and French authorities in the 19th century were concerned about the activities of marabouts in North Africa, and for the British, the fakirs in India. Popular belief in them was strong, and with their boasts of magical powers, they were a potential focus of resistance against colonial rule. In 1856, the French authorities in Algeria decided to employ Western stage magic to undermine the influence of the marabout. Their weapon of choice was the famed illusionist Jean-Eugène Robert-Houdin (1805–71), the man who later inspired the American escapologist Erik Weisz to call himself Houdini. As Houdin later explained,

> It was hoped, with reason, that my performances would lead Arabs to understand that the marabouts' trickery is naught but simple child's play... Naturally this entailed demonstrating our superiority in everything and showing that, as far as sorcerers are concerned, there is no match for the French.

Dressed smartly, as ever, in his usual Western evening dress, Houdin put on several performances for Algerian audiences, amongst them apparently some marabout. One of his most appropriate illusions for the task at hand was the well-known 'gun trick' in which the magician is shot at but amazingly remains unscathed, taking from his mouth, or an object close to the body, the bullet that had been marked in public view before being loaded into the gun. The authorities had been concerned by reports that some marabouts had demonstrated their invincibility by subjecting themselves to a suspiciously similar ordeal. During his first performance, a purported marabout ardently volunteered to fire the gun, only to be left awestruck at Houdin's unmagical skill. The press presented Houdin's trip as a triumph for colonial rationality: 'today the marabouts are totally discredited among the natives', announced one newspaper.

Early psychiatry

Witchcraft sceptics such as the French Catholic intellectual Michel de Montaigne (1533–92) argued that the tales of amazing magical feats that some people accused witches of, and to which some suspected witches confessed, were often the products of the imagination. After paying a visit to a group of elderly women convicted of witchcraft, Montaigne wrote: 'In the end, and in all honesty, I would have prescribed not hemlock but hellebore.' In other words, they deserved not death but cure. Quoting the Roman historian Titus Livy, Montaigne continued, 'Their case seemed to be more a matter of insane minds than of criminal behaviour.' In his book *De præstigiis dæmonum*, the Dutch physician Johann Weyer (1515–88) presented extensive arguments that witches' delusions regarding their magical powers were the result of fantastical dreams and hallucinations.

Weyer, della Porta, and others believed that some of these hallucinatory experiences were caused by the poisonous and narcotic plants that some supposed witches were thought to use in their ointments and rituals. Hemlock was one of them. It was these plants that gave them the sensation of having flown great distances. People who believed they had been bewitched could have also unwittingly ingested narcotic substances. Weyer mentions a woman who fed the labourers she employed with bread made with rye flour. After eating it, 'they became slightly mad' and fell into a long and profound sleep. When she stopped feeding them the rye bread, they recovered. The link was made, but what Weyer and the woman did not know was that they had probably ingested the fungus ergot that grows on rye. It contains hallucinogenic properties, which in the 20th century gave rise to LSD. The discovery of this fact has led to inflated claims that the fantasies of Sabbaths and being ridden by witches can all be explained by ergot poisoning. The main explanation for the confessions of diabolic orgies, as Weyer was well aware, was the torture that many accused witches were subjected to on the

Continent and in Scotland. Forced confessions elicited what torturers wanted to hear, shaped by leading questions.

Weyer and others identified the condition known as melancholy as a key source of magic beliefs. While this early modern medical category of mental illness included what we today call depression, it was also understood in a wider philosophical, literary, legal, and spiritual way. Hellebore was used to cure some of its symptoms, as well as to ward off witches and evil spirits that were thought able to inflict melancholy. Women, elderly ones in particular, were thought to be particularly prone to melancholy, and therefore more likely to believe that in their miserable reveries they met with the Devil, flew to sabbats, danced with the fairies, and caused magical harm to their neighbours. Weyer's *De præstigiis dæmonum* included a chapter on 'The distorted imagination of melancholics'. In it, he explained how

> Strange apparitions may thus be conceived in the imagination and generally shared with the visual spirits and humors through the medium of the optic nerve, so that these deluded women dare to affirm under threat of death that they have seen or done things which have never been seen and have never existed in reality.

The connections between women, mental disorder, and magic were reinforced by the 19th-century psychiatric profession. The pioneering French psychiatrist Jean-Martin Charcot (1825–93) and colleagues at the Salpêtrière women's asylum in Paris analysed the accounts of possession, witchcraft, and ecstatic experiences to be found in the witch trial material, and found direct analogies with the 'hysterical' symptoms of their female patients. The concept of *demonopathie*, the condition of possession as a form of insanity, was born. Charcot and the early psychiatric profession lauded Weyer as the first psychiatrist, a physician far ahead of his time. The fact that Weyer also believed in demonic intervention and that demons caused bodily harm was conveniently ignored.

6. ***Une leçon clinique à la Salpêtrière*** **(1887), by the artist André Brouillet (1857–1914). It depicts Charcot demonstrating hysteria at the Salpêtrière Hospital with the patient Blanche Wittmann (1859–1913), known as the 'Queen of Hysterics'**

The problem with these early attempts at psychologizing magic out of existence was that just too many people believed in it to be able to explain away magical belief and experience in terms of illusion, deception, credulity, optical trickery, drugs, melancholy, and hysteria. The 19th-century psychiatrists extrapolated from individual neurological experiences to create theories of societal pathologies born of religion and ignorance. They were exciting and bold ideas but nevertheless fantastical. Perhaps a deeper exploration into the subconscious would prove more convincing.

Freud

Sigmund Freud (1856–1939) was a master of the occult in the sense of exploring the hidden recesses of the mind. His interest in the witch trials, for instance, was aroused by his spell studying at the Salpêtrière with Charcot. Inspired by the latter, in his various works Freud employed the technique of 'retrospective medicine'; in other words, using historical cases to prove the universal and timeless nature of the psychoanalytic categories of dysfunction he identified in his patients. His studies of hysteria were much influenced by this. The problem with the method, though, at least as used by Freud, was that the cases chosen were highly selective and not necessarily as representative as he portrayed them to be. Furthermore, with regard to his work on witchcraft and hysteria, he conflated the condition of the possessed with that of accused witches, and largely ignored the fact that the witch confessions he used as analogues had been extracted by torture: they were not necessarily the fantasies of the witches, but those of the inquisitors. Whose subconscious was he really exploring?

Freud's views on magic and religion were framed by the evolutionary classification of magic as an expression of the earliest stage of primitive culture. Consequently, the continued belief in it was a survival, though of a psychological rather than cultural kind. In his works, Freud used the term 'magic' liberally, and particularly with reference to the power of words. Regarding his time with Charcot, for instance, he wrote of a 'magic that flowed from his looks and from his voice'. His own attempt to define it required him to make a fundamental distinction between 'sorcery' and 'magic', though he was aware of the problematic linguistic journey of the terms. So, for Freud, sorcery was 'essentially the art of influencing spirits by treating them in the same way as one would treat men in like circumstances'. Magic, on the other hand, 'disregards spirits and makes use of special procedures and not of everyday psychological methods'. Magic preceded sorcery in the evolutionary scale. Instead of being rooted in social interaction, magic was rooted in the individual emotional state: it was about the self, though not without social consequences.

Freud's psychoanalytic interpretation of magic was explained in most detail in his essay 'Animism, Magic and the Omnipotence of

Thoughts', which appeared as a chapter in his classic work *Totem and Taboo* (1913). Freud relied heavily on the work of E. B. Tylor, Frazer, and other contributors to the magic/religion/science debate, and worked his own ideas around their discourse on contagious and imitative magic. 'It will be easy to arrive at a satisfactory explanation of magic merely by carrying the associative theory further and deeper', Freud stated with supreme confidence. This he did by comparing the magic-enslaved egos of the primitives of the past with the mental processes of neurotics and the early development of children. All three groups exhibited a similar narcissistic trait, he postulated. Magic was based on the conviction of the omnipotence of their thought and absolute confidence in the power of their wishes. In short, magic was a self-delusion with thoughts substituted for reality. Theorizing more widely, or wildly, Freud conceived magic as a universal pre-Oedipal stage in cultural and mental evolution.

Several of the post-First World War generation of anthropologists found value in Freudian analysis. The Hungarian scholar Géza Róheim (1891–1953), who was a practitioner of both disciplines, stressed the sexual aspects of magical practices more than Freud, exploring the oral and anal aspects of frustration and eroticism. When it came to the origin of magic, he put the mother–child relationship at the heart of his theorizing. In a posthumously published essay, 'The Origin and Function of Magic', he explained how the original and perpetual magical principle derived from the omnipotent thoughts of the infant whose preverbal and verbal expressed desires were gratified by maternal response: in this sense, incantations were realized. Breaking from the evolutionary model, and thereby distancing himself from Freud, Róheim viewed magic as a liberating psychological force. It was not a survival of the primitive but a basic element of thought and the 'initial phase of any activity'.

While Róheim's psychoanalytical ideas were not taken seriously by anthropologists, Malinowski's engagement with Freudian theory was the subject of much attention. Malinowski was largely persuaded by Freud's psychosexual ideas of human behaviour, and his projection of them back into the distant past. They did not share the same sense of the trajectory of thought and culture, though. While Freud believed the 'illusion' of magic and religion would eventually wither in the age of science, Malinowski saw religion and magic as an essential part of the human condition – past, present, and future. As he wrote in his essay 'Magic, Science and Religion', 'We find magic an invariable adjunct of all important activities. I think we must see in it the embodiment of the sublime folly of hope.'

The superstitious mind

Psychologists have often been more comfortable dealing with the category of 'superstition' than 'magic'. They have generally engaged with anthropological concepts such as 'magical worldview' only when it comes to children's mental development. Jean Piaget (1896–1980) was a pioneer in this field of psychology. In a series of books looking at children's perception of reality, logic, and how they interpret physical causation, he explored their development through several animistic and magical stages of thought. We shall return to this research on 'magical thinking' in the final chapter.

There are a couple of reasons for the psychologists' preference for talking 'superstition' with regard to *adult* beliefs. As a discipline keen to be accepted as a science, they preferred to use a descriptor that denoted, more clearly than the diffuse cultural use of 'magic', a set of beliefs that were, in psychologist Gustav Jahoda's words, 'clearly and *demonstrably* false'. Belief in them was, therefore, by inference, expressive of atypical psychological behaviour. Jahoda, who wrote an influential text on the *Psychology of Superstition* (1969), was well aware, though, that some 'superstitions' were difficult to prove false by science, and that falsity itself is 'always relative to a given state of knowledge'. So defining superstition in a modern, secular context can be just as slippery as magic. The two terms often end up being used as synonyms in psychological texts, even if superstition is the headline concept.

A second reason for working with 'superstition' concerns the nature of psychology research. Questionnaires are an important tool for understanding the psychology of belief. For them to be successful, it is obviously important that the respondents understand what is being asked. People have a basic, shared understanding of what 'superstition' means, and a general idea of what constitutes superstitious behaviour. Ask simply about 'magic', and confusion is likely over what type of magic is meant. So, at this basic level, ask people, 'Are you superstitious?' and it is likely that you will get a significantly bigger 'Yes' response than if you asked them 'Do you believe in magic?' Psychological surveys tend to focus on a limited set of 'common superstitions' widely recognized across cultures, countries, and religions, and which are uncomplicated in their purpose – generally to ensure good luck and avoid bad luck. Do you knock on wood? Avoid walking under ladders? Cross your fingers? The results have been interpreted as showing that 'superstitious' belief is linked to levels of personal anxiety and poor psychological adjustment. One problem with such questionnaires, though, is that they are often concerned with negative superstitions such as 'breaking a mirror causes bad luck'. It has been argued that surveys of positive superstitions, such as the wearing of lucky charms, could produce results that lead to different psychological diagnoses.

There are certainly some links between magical thinking, ritual, and psychological disorder. Obsessive-compulsive disorder (OCD) is the most obvious example. Sufferers engage in repetitive activities, such as checking a door is closed, or avoidance mannerisms, such as not walking on cracks in the paving, out of a fear that failing to carry out these rituals will lead to some misfortune. The imagined misfortune is sometimes specific, such as the death of a family member, but is often ill-defined. OCD sufferers do not, however, carry out their rituals to promote good fortune. Yet superstition, as understood by psychologists, cannot be explained as a form of psychopathology more generally. It is too pervasive as both a belief and a practice.

Psychologists' implicit engagement with magic, and their opaque conception of it, is also encapsulated in the language of the 'paranormal' or the 'psychical'. A widely used tool in this field of psychological research is the Paranormal Belief Scale (PBS) developed in the 1980s and revised in the early 2000s. For the PBS, the working definition of paranormal phenomena is that, if genuine, they 'would violate basic limiting principles of science'. Magic could be defined in the same way. But for the reasons stated above, there is no category of 'magic' in the PBS, or in a Chinese version of it developed to suit different cultural beliefs. The seven categories of paranormal belief in the PBR are: traditional religious belief, psi, witchcraft, superstition, spiritualism, extraordinary life forms, and precognition. The one question pertaining to magic, 'Black magic really exists', is a subscale of 'witchcraft'. Presumably the inference is meant to be that 'black magic' is evil, and by association concerned with belief in Satanic action. Interestingly, the concept of magic is bolstered in the revised version of the PBS. Two items in the original scale pertaining to the belief in voodoo were replaced because the notion was not familiar in many cultures. One was replaced with, 'Through the use of formulas and incantations, it is possible to cast spells on persons.' This is certainly a statement that can be globally understood, as we shall now find out.

Chapter 4
Writing magic

The power of the word is one of the contested boundaries between magic and religion. Most of the world's sacred religious texts mention magic. The Koran refers to *sihr* some sixty times in contexts, as an Egyptian Islamic 'Guideline for the people' explains, 'from the bizarre and unusual to the attracting of attention and the occasioning of astonishment'. Forty-eight citations concerning amulets have been identified in the Babylonian Talmud, one of two compilations of ancient Jewish law and custom. Both the Old and New Testaments contain many references to magical practices, and their interpretation has caused controversy in Judaism and from the early days of the Christian faith. In these religions, authority depends completely on the written word, the literary record of the sayings of the prophets and their followers. The possession of them was an act of worship in itself. For much of the history of these religions, though, very few people possessed copies of the sacred texts, let alone had the education to read them. Access was restricted, often deliberately. In the 'wrong hands', holy texts could be misinterpreted and mistranslated. They could be used to support magic and magicians. They could also be used to make magic.

Using religious texts

When does the recitation of Koranic verses tip over from licit devotion to *shirk* or *sihr*? How to avoid using the Koran in magical ways? This is what the Wahabbi movement accuses Sufism of doing with its repetitive chanting of Koranic verses. Numerous guides have been produced for popular consumption providing 'correct' uses of the Koran to counteract djinns, and for healing and protection. *The Sword against Black Magic and Evil Magicians*, by Wahid Ibn Abdessalam Bali, is one such contemporary guide that has been through numerous editions across the Arabic world, and has also been published in cheap French and English editions to widen its teachings. Bali, who is a Saudi scholar of Wahhabi persuasion, has written several texts dealing with combating *sihr* and djinns. *Sword against Black Magic* provides advice on dealing with the evil eye, sexual problems, lunacy, illness, and bad dreams caused by *sihr*. Bali fully accepts that *sihr* is based on demonic action. His aim is to demonstrate that only through the Koran and not through the resort to counter-magic or magical practitioners can *sihr* be combated. He reports that it is generally accepted that the punishment for practising *sihr* is death. There are two types of *an-nushra* – curing a person of *sihr*. Treating *sihr* with *sihr*, by calling upon djinns, for example, is the work of Satan, but treating *sihr* with the Koran is permitted.

But the Koran is nevertheless widely used in what could be seen as incorrect ways. To counteract the bodily influence of malign spirits, for instance, some Islamic healers recite the opening chapter of the Koran, the *Fātiha*, blowing the words on the victim and then anointing them with spittle. A popular book of healing, the *Tibb-ul-Nabbi* or *Medicine of the Prophet*, by the 15th-century scholar Al-Suyútí, mentions a charm whereby water over which verses of the Koran have been recited was used by the sick for washing themselves. Al-Suyútí notes, though, that a close companion of Muhammad described this practice as an abomination. Nevertheless, some Muslim communities in Africa, such as the Berti of Darfur, employ the similar custom of drinking the Koran. The holy men healers of the Berti, known as *fakis*, who have been to Koranic schools and memorized the Koran, practise this ritual of 'erasure'. They write certain Koranic verses, chosen depending on the nature of the ailment, on a wooden slate with ink made of soot and gum arabic. This verse is then washed off and given to the patient. An erasure used against the evil eye runs as follows:

> Say: He is God,
> The One and Only;
> God, the Eternal, Absolute
> He begetteth not,
> Nor is He begotten;
> And there is none
> Like unto Him.

The Koran can be used for magical purposes beyond personal health and protection. One ritual for discovering buried treasure requires that verse 9 of sura 3, and all of sura 95, be written on paper and attached to the neck of a white cockerel bearing a double comb. The bird is let loose, and if it stands in a particular place and then dies the next day, treasure is buried at that spot.

In India, the Atharvaveda, the fourth book of the holy Vedas, is, depending on one's point of view, the most valuable or pernicious source of Hindu magical healing and protection. Discussion on the Atharvaveda has been shaped by the old magic/religion/science debate, with it being repeatedly stated that because of its spells and charms it must, in origin, be the most ancient of the Vedic texts. It contains some 730 exorcisms, healing hymns, and poetic charms, with accompanying rituals to counter diseases and demons, for health and long life, the prevention of misfortune, and aid in battle. They have numerous parallels with those charms found in magic texts from the ancient Mediterranean world and medieval Europe. We find, for example, sympathetic magic, the use of ritual repetition, and rhetoric questions. As in European tradition, iron is recommended as a potent general protection against evil spirits. Diseases are caused by a myriad of gods, demons, and spirits. Many of the charms require the use of healing plants either as amulets or burned for purification and expelling. Here is one of the more simple charms to ward off evil:

> Let me go, O evil; being powerful, take thou pity on us! Set me, O evil, unharmed, into the world of happiness!
>
> If, O evil, thou dost not abandon us, then do we abandon thee at the fork of the road. May evil follow after another (man)!
>
> Away from us may thousand-eyed, immortal (evil) dwell! Him whom we hate may it strike, and him whom we hate do thou surely smite!

The Atharvaveda is not central to the Vedic texts, though, so unlike the use of the Christian Bible or the Muslim Koran, it can be rejected or ignored without necessarily undermining the other three Vedas. Those campaigning to rationalize Hinduism see it as a pernicious source of magic. As one recent cultural history of India explained: 'In the Atharvaveda a religion of magic with its childish reliance on sorcery and witchcraft, takes the place of purer Vedic religion.'

The Buddhist *dhāranī-sūtras*, composed in medieval China in the 4th and 5th centuries CE, should also be mentioned in this respect. Like the Atharvaveda, these books of spells have long had a dubious position within the orthodox canon of Buddhist texts. One example is the *Kuan-ting ching*, or *Book of Consecration*. It contains twelve *sūtras* or formulas with titles such as 'Spells of the 72,000 Spirit-kings' and 'Protective Spells of the Hundred-knotted Spirit-kings', which deal with divination, the exorcism of disease-demons, the protection of tombs and homes, and also bewitchment. As stated in the *Book*, there were those who called upon the gods of the moon, sun, and mountains, and the demons of the trees, to 'enter into pacts with them in order to realize all sorts of bewitchments. They make use of peoples' names, fabricate effigies of them, creating talismans and spells whose aim is to bewitch them'. The text itself was thought to have innate protective powers.

The Jewish Torah and the Christian New Testament contain a range of people who became associated with magical knowledge such as Moses, Solomon, and Simon Magus. Some purported sources of magic are more surprising. There are Coptic magic spells and books attributed to the Virgin Mary. One such spell begins:

> This is the 21st prayer (that) the Virgin Mary spoke (on) the day (of) her falling asleep. It restrains all the powers of the adversary (and) it cures every disease and every sickness, in peace, Amen.

Many examples can be found from the early centuries AD of passages from the Torah/Old Testament being recited for healing or protective purposes. Psalm 91, for instance, was long employed as an anti-demonic. A 14th-century manuscript, the *Sefer Gematriaot*, contains a long list of the magical uses of biblical verses. For protection at night, it recommends reciting Genesis 49:18, and to be rendered invisible, Genesis 19:11. As with the Koran, guides circulated as to the secret power of these holy words. One of the most enduringly popular Jewish texts was the *Sepher Shimmush Tehillim*, which perhaps dates back to the late 1st millennium. It provides instructions on the practical power of the Psalms, and claims 'The entire Torah is composed of the names of God, and in consequence it has the property of saving and protecting man.'

The Christian Bible was also potent as a physical object. In Europe, examples are found of it being kept under pillows for protection at night, pages of it were ingested to cure sickness, and it was also used in various divinatory rituals. More so than other literary religions, Christian legends and apocrypha played a major part in generating magic. The apocrypha – Christian texts and stories that are not recognized by the Churches but which detail the lives and sayings of biblical characters – formed the basis of protective charms that circulated widely across Europe from the medieval period through to the 20th century. They involve accounts, for example, of the Three Wise Men, the names of whom in Western Christianity, Caspar, Melchior, and Balthasar, derive from apocrypha not the Bible. Their names are widely cited in the archive of incantations and charms, and in Bohemia the initials CMB were chalked on doors as protection. Perhaps the most sensational examples of apocryphal magic are the Heavenly or Celestial Letters that purport to be communications from Jesus to King Abgar V (died *c.* 50 CE) of Edessa, in southern Turkey. They date back as early as the 4th century, and continued to be pasted on the walls of English labourers' cottages and kept in the pockets of soldiers in the First World War trenches for protection one and half thousand years later.

Amulets and talismans

In all religions with a literary foundation, holy texts are used to create talismans and amulets that are worn for protection, healing, and good fortune. An agent, a magician, is usually required to effect the process, either through innate or learned power. Babylonian clay amulets in cuneiform dating back to the early 1st millennium BCE have been discovered that call upon the gods Marduk, Erra, and Išum, to protect houses from the plague. Most were based on the epic poem of Erra (the goddess of plague and chaos), the earliest surviving fragments of which date to around 800 BCE. One example runs as follows:

> O Marduk, wisest of the gods, Era, most valiant of the gods, Išum, in charge of the streets, Seven Gods, heroes who cannot be equalled, have mercy on me, PN, son of his (personal) god, your respectful worshiper, in this epidemic, this calamity, this scourge, the raging of Era, the pestilence, ... of the strong Era, and then I will sing your praise for all time to come to all mankind.

Many such examples of literary amulets, on papyrus, pots, clay, lead, leather, and stones, have been recorded from ancient Egypt, Greece, and Rome.

It was not just the holy power of the words but the surfaces on which they were written that made amulets efficacious. As well as parchment, Koranic verses were written on silver, copper, iron, stones, white muslin, camel bones, unleavened bread, and the shoulder blades of sheep. The type of writing medium used also had magical significance. Liquids such as mint juice, honey, saffron, musk, and rose water all had distinct properties. Like the Bible, the Koran was and is used as a talisman in itself. Kept under the pillow, it wards off witches from harming women in childbirth, and tiny editions kept in a gold or silver box are worn around the neck for protection. Today, tiny editions of the Koran can be found displayed on the dashboards or back windows of cars to protect against accidents.

A group of instructional texts on creating Koranic amulets, written in faltering Arabic, were brought from the Guinea coast of the Ashanti Empire in West Africa to Denmark in 1826. They are a rare archive of the process by which non-Islamic, oral African societies came to value the written magical power of the Koran introduced to them by traders from the north. One of the amulets for military purposes advises:

> Whoever wants victory in war should write the following and then wash it into a container. Some gold and silver should be put in it and then wash your body with it. Write *Ayat al-Kursi* twelve thousand times. Also write *Surat al-Kawthar* three hundred times. Do all these in secrecy without people knowing your intentions.

Considerable quantities of gold no doubt exchanged hands between Koranic amulet vendors and the Ashanti, complementing but not supplanting their indigenous corpus of magical practices.

Modern Nigeria, which has a substantial Muslim and Christian population, provides a good example of how the Koran and the Bible are used for the same magical purposes. A visitor to a market in Maiduguri in northern Nigeria in the 1930s came across a charm-seller who sold passages from the Koran written on pieces of paper and placed in leather pouches to be worn against scorpions, snakes, or the spear of an enemy. And a recent survey of livestock healing in the north found that 35% of the herdsmen questioned reported using the Koran for protection, either reading verses over their animals or attaching to them written verses. Moving south, a study of the Ibibio tribe of southern Nigeria in the early 1980s showed how Western Christian evangelism had fostered the talismanic use of the Bible. *Faith*, the monthly magazine of the American Life-Study Fellowship, an organization founded in 1939 and based in Connecticut, provided lists of potent biblical passages that were adopted by Ibibios as protection from witchcraft when written down on parchment from sacred animals. Similar amulets of biblical or pseudo-Hebraic origin were also purchased from the Chicago mail-order magical supplies company founded in the early 20th century by the occult entrepreneur William Lauron Delaurence. The company had agents in several west Nigerian towns.

The *mezuzah* is perhaps the best known and most widely used of Judaic amulets. It is not meant to be used or interpreted as protective magic, of course. It consists of a wooden, metal, or ceramic container in which is kept a scroll of parchment containing two passages from Deuteronomy on one side and the word '*Shaddai*' (Almighty) on the other. It is attached to the doorpost of the main entrance of the home (*mezuzah* means doorpost). From a theological point of view, it represents an act of communal unity and serves to remind Jews of their obligations each time they leave and enter their homes. In practice, many Jews, including some medieval rabbis, used it as a protective amulet warding off evil spirits and unwelcome people from the home. Occult signs and angelic names were sometimes added to the parchment to enhance its magical properties. There is evidence that during the medieval and early modern period, *mezuzahs* were also sought after by Christians as potent amulets.

Hebrew passages from the Torah and the Psalms were also carried for the prevention of disease. *Halakah* (Jewish law) proscribes using words from the Torah for curing the sick, with the exception of saving life, but allows it for *preventing* disease and evil. But rabbinical sanction has been given for the initials of words and sentences from the Torah to be used curatively. This gave rise to the use of amulets bearing holy Hebraic acronyms. A potent example is '*Ibka Yazai Bamai*' from Psalm 69, 7. In the early 1990s, an Israeli doctor reported that quite a few of his patients wore such amulets produced by professional amulet vendors.

Word squares, palindromes, and anagrams based on holy words such as the Christian 'Pater Noster' also accrued potency. The growing or diminishing word was an ancient and pervasive aspect of literary talismans, found in many magic cultures and not dependent on holy texts. The most famous example is the diminishing ABRACADABRA, usually depicted in a triangular form ending with 'a'.

ABRACADABRA
ABRACADABR
ABRACADAB
ABRACADA
ABRACAD
ABRACA
ABRAC
ABRA
ABR
AB
A

It was used as an amulet in the Roman world, was carried on scraps of paper during the London plague of 1665, and continued to be used in European popular magic into the 20th century, before losing its potency and becoming an everyday word of fun.

Its origin remains obscure, with one suggestion being that it derives from the Hebrew '*Ha-Brachah-dabarah*' (Name of the Blessed). Numerous other diminishing formulations have been concocted over the centuries. Some 19th-century Danish books of magic contained a diminishing triangle of the obscure word KALEMARIS. Today, the followers of the Ukrainian mystic Rabbi Nachman (1772–1810), whose tomb in Uman (Ukraine) became a popular pilgrimage destination, use protective amulets playing on his name, the word '*na*' meaning 'to travel', and his resting place. It runs as follows: 'NA, NACH, NACHMA, NACHMAN, ME-UMAN'. This formula can be found adorning cars and buildings in Israel to ensure safe journeys and general good fortune.

This leads us on to letter magic. Specific Hebraic or Arabic letters are thought to be imbued with or to attract power. In formal worship, the Torah is learned and read in Hebrew and the Koran in Arabic; they are, therefore, in essence, sacred languages. This is amplified in Islamic populations whose first language is not Arabic, and their only interaction with it is through the Koran. No wonder then that letters accrued magical properties. The 14th-century Arab Muslim scholar Ibn Khaldūn considered letter magic, which was particularly associated with Sufism, as a form of natural magic, or *sīmyā*. The 28 letters were infused with spiritual powers that 'encompass the secrets existing in the worlds'. Each was attributed to one of the four elements. So letters aligned with water were potent in curing fevers. Today, African marabouts use Arabic letters in their charms, mixing them with magic signs, writing them backwards or upside down.

The power of the letter in Jewish Kabbalah is better known in the Western magical tradition, having been developed by Jewish scholars in medieval Spain and southern France. Drawing upon esoteric notions apparent in Judaism a millennium earlier, the medieval Kabbalah tradition was inspired by a purportedly re-discovered text (a familiar theme in esoteric magic) named

7. Malayan spell intended to curse its recipient. The Arabic letters around the human figure are incantations written in the mysterious language of the djinns

the *Sefer Zohar*, or *Book of Splendour*, which was written down in Aramaic and Hebrew in 13th-century Spain. Its promoter, Moshe (Moses) de Leon, claimed dubiously that it was the work of a rabbi in 2nd-century CE Roman Palestine. The *Zohar* provides a mystical interpretation of the Torah and inspires a

8. A Syrian amulet in the form of a silver hand bearing Hebraic characters. Known as the *Hamsa*, or Hand of Fatima, in Arabic cultures, and *Hamesh*, or Hand of Miriam, amongst Jews, in North Africa and the Middle East such amulets have long been used to ward off the evil eye

transcendent purpose for worship. Kabbalah is complex, but central to it as a *practice* is the use of the 22 letters of the Hebrew alphabet (all consonants). Every letter has a hidden meaning and a numerical representation. Together, they represent the creative force of God and the building blocks of the world. Once understood, they can be used in different permutations to achieve wisdom and spiritual unity. For some, they could also be used in magical formulae, harnessing divine emanations and the realm of spirits for practical results. During the 16th century, the Kabbalah was also absorbed into Christian occult philosophy and Neoplatonic magic. As a result, real and pseudo-Hebraic letters litter the pages of the many manuscript and printed books of magic that circulated from the Renaissance period onwards.

Books of magic

So far, we have explored the centrality of religious texts to the notion of words as magical and writing as a magical act. But from early antiquity onwards, compilations of rituals, conjurations, spells, and magical secrets circulated that operated outside the boundaries of official religion. There are those that can be categorized as grimoires due to their inclusion of conjurations and adjurations of gods, angels, demons, or other spirits. The term 'grimoire' to describe such books of magic only came into regular usage in 18th-century France, and was subsequently widely adopted in English literature. Then there are magic books that sought to show how to exploit the occult mysteries of the natural world. Grimoires usually contained both these natural and spiritual forms of magic.

The origins of these handbooks or manuals of magic date right back to early antiquity. Compilations of spells and incantations recorded on clay tablets have been found at Middle Eastern archaeological sites dating to the early centuries of the 1st millennium BCE. Their subsequent development rested on the introduction of new literary technologies. At the same time, new technologies became imbued with magical properties. This was a potent combination. So the use of papyrus as a writing surface enabled metres of text to be rolled up into a portable record of information. This allowed coherent, sequential, explanatory handbooks of magic to be stored and passed on. An entire body of accumulated magical wisdom could be encoded and transported by one person. Papyrus also allowed for different inks with different properties to be used for magical effect.

Leather had also been used to write on as far back as the 3rd millennium BCE in Egypt, but the creation of parchment from animal skin, which requires a more complex procedure to produce its far superior writing surface, was only developed during the 3rd century BCE. Whereas papyrus was made from the sedge plant of the same name that grew in the Nile Delta, there were no environmental or geographical restrictions to the production of parchment. This opened up new avenues for magical activity. From a practical point of view, parchment could be written on on both sides and individual pages stitched together; so more on information could be packed into smaller portable units. The scroll was dead and the book of magic was born. The impact on religion as well as magic was revolutionary. The successful spread of the evangelical religions of Christianity and Islam was based upon the parchment book, and, as we have seen, the spread of the Bible and Koran became integral to magical practices wherever these religions were adopted.

Magic books exist in other ancient literary cultures, though they were not necessarily produced from parchment due to the sacred ideas of certain religions. Examples of 'religious' texts, such as the Hindu Atharvaveda and Buddhist *dhāranī-sūtras*, have already been noted. The discovery of what are known as the Shui-hu-ti 'daybooks', or almanacs, by archaeologists in 1975 provides an important insight into magic in China at the end of the Warring States period during the 3rd century BCE. They were found amongst a number of legal texts written on bamboo slips in a tomb dated to around 220 BCE at Shui-hu-ti, in Hupei province. The daybooks contain a mix of astrological, divinatory, and magical advice. They reveal the important role of ghosts in early Chinese popular religion, and provide spells for dealing with them. So:

> When a dog continuously enters a person's house at night, seizing the husband and sporting with the woman, and it cannot be caught, it is a sacred dog disguised as a ghost. Use the bark of a mulberry tree... roast it and eat it. This will stop it.

From the 12th century onwards, grimoires expanded in number, range, and cultural influence across Europe and the Mediterranean world. In Christian kingdoms, monasteries were centres of production and reproduction, and the clergy the biggest market. Towards the end of the medieval period, in the 15th century, the expanding legal and medical professions created a larger readership for the almost exclusively Latin grimoires with their smattering of Hebrew and Greek. There were books with titles such as 'The Book of Angels, Rings, Characters and Images of the Planets', the 'Notory Art' attributed to Solomon, and 'The Sworn Book of Honorius of Thebes'. Pseudo-authorship had long been a hallmark of the magic book. Indeed, those great names of medieval learning, the Englishman Roger Bacon, and his German contemporary Albertus Magnus of Cologne, were given the dubious honour of having books of demonic and natural magic named after them. In Arabic magic literature, the most influential texts were the *Ghāyat al-Hakīm* or *Picatrix*, which contained ritual conjurations and astral magic, and the works of two very real scholars, the 13th-century *Shams al-ma'ārif* ('Illumination of Knowledge') by Ahmad bin Ali al-Buni, and those of the 9th-century Iraqi astral magician Abū Yūsuf al-Kindi. His literary work provided a hugely valuable repository of ancient Greek occult thought for European scholars and magicians.

The printing of magical knowledge inhibits important aspects of the literary magic tradition. The magical process of transcription and compilation was depersonalized, the use of consecrated pens and writing fluids rendered redundant. Although from the early days of printing in the late 15th century, it was possible to print on fine-quality parchment, it was time-consuming and expensive. The paper in printed books was now almost exclusively made from linen and cotton rags. But printing did not kill off the potency of the literary magic tradition. If anything, it revolutionized it by increasing access to a world of magic that had once been the preserve of a select few. Magic became a commercial prospect as never before. Books of natural magic, such as that attributed to Albertus Magnus, were amongst the earliest best-sellers. Then the work of German Renaissance occult philosophers such as Cornelius Agrippa began to appear. It was in the 18th century, though, the heart of the so-called 'Age of Enlightenment', that a democratic revolution occurred in the history of literary magic. In France, thousands of illicit cheap books of natural and ritual magic poured from the presses and found their way into the hands of the poor for the very first time. One of the most notorious, the *Grand grimoire*, even advised on how to conjure up the Devil. These French editions would find their way into Spain, Italy, German lands, and French territories in the Caribbean and Indian Ocean.

Elsewhere, the *Shimmush Tehillim* appeared numerous times in cheap print from the late 18th century, and achieved further widespread use in America due to its inclusion in a German translation of what was entitled the *Sixth and Seventh Books of Moses*. In North Africa, Al-Suyúti's *Tibb-ul-Nabbi*, which had circulated widely for several centuries in manuscript, achieved a much wider reach in the 19th century through cheap print editions. Now its Koranic advice on healing and amulets, such as that eating seven ajwa dates (the Prophet's favourite) for breakfast warded off *sihr* and harm for the day, were available more widely. Several editions were published in Cairo, Tehran, and Bombay in the 1870s and 1880s. Popular print versions of al-Buni's *Shams al-ma'arif al-kubra* were sold at street stalls from Morocco to Egypt and Yemen. Yet, despite widespread access to such cheap magic literature, the ability to use books of magic successfully was still thought to be primarily the preserve of certain talented individuals.

Chapter 5
Practising magic

From a popular perspective, magic is an action. For it to exist, people have to perform it, occasionally unwittingly (as with the evil eye) but generally deliberately. Some magic can be performed by everyone. This open-access magic is truly popular in that it is in no way dependent on religion, magicians, or literacy. Knowledge is passed down orally within families and communities. But I know of no culture across the globe, past and present, which did not require specialists. As I intimated at the end of the last chapter, the mere possession of magical knowledge was not the only quality required to enable the successful practice of magic.

Global comparisons

I could go on for hundreds of pages providing examples of similar magical practices from cultures around the globe and across time. There are plenty to be found. One good example is the creation and mutilation of images of people to enact harm. Archaeologists have found examples from the ancient world. We saw it mentioned in a medieval Chinese text in the last chapter, it is described in the European witch trial records, and is well recorded in Africa, Asia, and the Americas. Today, it has iconic status as the voodoo doll, sold as a commercial product, into which pins are stuck. Another more obscure example concerns a ritual for detecting thieves. A method employed by Muslims in India involved the magician writing the names of suspected people on slips of paper. These were then made into balls or pills by mixing them with flour paste. When placed in a water vessel, the ball with the name of the thief rose to the surface first. We find a similar procedure recorded from medieval England, with names encased in clay balls.

Such global analogues are fascinating, but what do they mean? Do they indicate a basic set of practices and rituals that date back to a formative period in human prehistoric culture and religious practice? This is essentially what the likes of Tylor and Frazer concluded, and it is from such comparisons that they constructed their theories of primitive culture. Others, likewise, identified similar rituals and customs across the globe from which they re-constructed what they considered to be the core concept behind the very first religion, such as sun or earth mother worship. As we have seen, these early social science theories, and the deductions behind them, have been undermined. But from the impressive corpus of comparative ethnographic materials that were gathered valuable concepts emerged. One of these was Frazer's identification of the law of sympathy as a key element of magic.

Sympathetic magic is certainly a universal principle that derives from the basic association of ideas. At its simplest, it means 'like affects like'. The voodoo doll is an example. Stick pins in the leg of the doll representing your intended victim, and your victim will be made lame. Stick a pin in its eye, and the victim will go blind. Paintings and photographs have been used in the same way. The act of using images for this purpose has been described as 'magical mimesis', *mimesis* being an ancient Greek term meaning 'to imitate', and was used primarily in the philosophical sense of the artistic representation of the physical world. In magical terms, anthropologists have used it to describe the attempt 'not only to express but to manipulate reality by means of its image'.

9. A terracotta figurine pierced by 13 nails, from a 3rd- or 4th-century Egyptian assemblage. It was placed in an earthenware pot along with a lead tablet bearing a love spell invoking demons

Marcel Mauss criticized Frazer for being overly dogmatic in proposing that the law of sympathy was a defining characteristic of magic but not religion. After all, what is the wearing or making of the sign of the Christian cross if not an act of sympathetic association? Mauss also rightly observed that sympathy did not explain all magical rites. Still, the examples from past and present are myriad. Much dream interpretation is based on sympathetic associations, for example. Let us take a peek at a dreambook from late antiquity called the 'Oneirocriticon of Astrampsychus'. It tells us that 'if you dream of dead people, you will experience the death of your affairs', 'if wasps appear, they are injuries inflicted by enemies', and that if you dream of sitting naked 'you will be stripped of your property'.

We find examples of sympathetic magic amongst the Bellacoola indigenous peoples of the Pacific coast of Canada. A bearskin was thrown over baby boys to make them grow up strong, and the warm limbs of a recently dead beaver – that most industrious of animals – were applied to baby girls so that they too would grow up with the same attribute. In Arabic cultures past and present, the scorpion was generally associated with evil, but because of its deadliness, it also served as a force of sympathetic protection. Beadwork amulets depicting scorpions were carried on the body and hung above doorways to ward off other scorpions and also the evil eye. The 13th-century Andalusian physician Ibn al-Baitar recommended a compress of the seeds of a certain plant, the leaves and seeds of which resembled a scorpion's tail, as a cure for scorpion bites.

The doctrine of signatures, the idea that the physical appearance of a plant bore a signature, in its colour or shape, indicative of its healing properties, underpinned much herbal medicine from the ancient world onwards. It was integral to European medicine through to the 18th century thanks to its espousal by the founding fathers of medical theory, the Roman physicians Dioscorides (*c.* 40–90) and Galen (*c.* 129–216). So the grey, moist liverwort was, as its name suggests, thought to be beneficial for liver disease because its colour and shape were similar to those of the liver. Plants with yellow flowers such as celandine were thought to counter the condition known as jaundice, which gives a yellow tinge to the skin. The doctrine of signatures can be considered as an aspect of natural magic, the discovery of the hidden properties in nature, but also has a non-magical aspect in terms of homeopathic medicine.

The concept of sympathetic magic has also been used to interpret the meaning of prehistoric art. Was it art for art's sake? Analogies suggested not. Frazer reported, for instance, how the Warramunga aborigines of Australia attempted to increase the number of emus by painting representations of them on the ground, depicting the most prized parts, the fat and the eggs, in particular. The men sat and sang around the painting and then some adorned themselves with headdresses to mimic the long neck and small head of the bird. It seemed reasonable to then compare such practices to European Palaeolithic cave art with their representations of hunting scenes. The depiction of horses, deer, and mammoths, perhaps pregnant, were intended to increase the number of such animals desired by hunter-gatherers, or to enhance their hunting success. The portrayal of dangerous animals was intended to diminish their threat. These interpretations have been undermined in recent decades, though. Critics pointed out, for example, that if the artists' intention was sympathetic hunting magic, then surely the animals would have been represented inflicted with arrows or spears, and the fertility of animals more overtly depicted. The sympathetic magic argument is not entirely redundant, though. One of the problems in rock art studies has been an implicit or explicit conception of all rock art as being part of a 'primitive' culture. Rock art across the globe may share similar features, but need not share the same meaning. Besides, some hunter-gather rock art is a few hundred years old and some over 40,000 years old. Studies of rock art in California depicting a figure shooting an arrow at another has parallels in ethnographic records regarding image magic amongst Native American peoples in the region.

Contagious magic is another aspect of the law of sympathy. When things have been in contact with each other, a link remains between them. The classic example is the hair of the dog, whereby it was thought that putting hair from the offending dog on the bite wound would cure rabies. Many other examples can be found. In British folk belief, putting a nail into a witch's footprint could break his or her spell. Another idea is that the possession of clothing or parts of the body can give you influence over their owner. In many cultures, there are concerns about hair or teeth getting into the wrong hands. In 1940s Liberia, a story was recorded about a houseboy who carefully retrieved all the nail clippings from a missionary's wastebasket and proudly returned them to him, assuring that no one could now cause him harm. This was because of the practice of taking the hair or discarded clothing of an enemy and secreting them in a tree or burying them in a hole while muttering some incantation. This charm was not intended to kill but rather to impede people so that they failed in their work or experienced repeated bad luck. In Western countries, so-called 'psychic detectives' say they require an item of a dead or missing person's clothing to be able to activate their clairvoyance.

The magical transference of disease was an act of contagious magic common in many cultures past and present. Ailments believed to be caused naturally and supernaturally could not be destroyed, and so the only means of cure was to pass on the ailments to others through some ritual act. In a sense, this notion is also an example of 'limited good' theory. A wart cure from North Carolina illustrates the process well: 'take an Irish potato, cut it up, rub it on the warts, put it in a sack and put it in a fork in the road. The first one who picks it up will have your warts; yours will disappear.' Decades before Frazer theorized about sympathetic magic, Joseph Ennemoser had discussed disease transference in a chapter on 'sympathetic superstitions'. He gave a Dutch example for curing the ague, or malaria:

> whoever has the ague, let him go early in the morning to an old willow tree, tie three knots in a branch, and say, 'Good morning old

one! I give thee the cold; good morning, old one!' You must then make a speedy exit.

As this ritual suggests, diseases did not have to be transferred to other humans. Ritually washing off the disease in flowing water or transferring it to animals could avoid such antisocial behaviour.

The professionals

In every recorded culture, there have been individuals who made a living by servicing the magical needs of the people. Like every aspect of magic, a global exploration of the world of magicians, who they were and are, what they did, and how they were perceived, could easily take up hundreds of pages and still only scratch the surface of the richness and meaning of magical practice. Here I can only provide some representative sketches. First, let me crudely divide magic specialists into religious and lay categories.

As we saw in the Introduction, holy men, the official or popular representatives of a religion, have always been associated with magic – particularly if we accept one definition of magic as the application of religious worship to solve everyday practical problems. The title 'priest-magician' has usually been applied to the religious officials of antiquity, primarily those of ancient Egypt. But the priest as magician lived on the monotheisms that developed later. The marabouts of African Islam have already been mentioned in this respect. The 'true' marabouts gain their popular esteem through being scholars and teachers of the Koran. It is their knowledge of the holy book, and how to use it for their community, that gives them their powers. When people in parts of Senegal have had a bit of good luck, they say, 'you've got a good marabout'.

A 19th-century Senegalese marabout named Amadou Bamba provides a good illustration of how they built their reputation.

First, he came from several generations of respected marabout. His father taught local children and married into the family of a tribal king. After his father's death, Bamba took his place in the king's entourage. When the king died in battle in 1886, Bamba returned to one of his ancestral homes and set up a *Tariqa* (Sufi school of instruction). He travelled the region preaching to locals that his Koranic powers were greater than their indigenous spirits. Once his reputation had grown in sufficient stature, he stopped his wanderings and prospered as clients now travelled to see him. But the power went to his head and he ceased to teach the local children, while his political ambitions concerned the French authorities. In 1895, he was deported to Gabon for seven years' exile. On his return, thousands of pilgrims flocked to see him. Bamba was at the pinnacle of the profession, and all marabouts were not equal in the eyes of the people. Reputations varied, and people would travel long distances to see a famed marabout rather than their inferior local one.

The Catholic and Orthodox priesthood has long fulfilled a similar role in Christianity. The Roman Catholic priest possessed divine privilege through the sacrament of ordination – he was the sole representative of God in his parish. Furthermore, like the marabout, until the modern era he was amongst the very few people who had access to the Holy Book. The Catholic Bible or Latin Vulgate was not meant to be read by the laity. It was the role of priests to interpret it for the people. This gave them control over the role of bodily and spiritual healing. This was backed up by an array of other potentially magical resources under their control, such as holy water, blessed herbs, the rite of exorcism, and rosaries. While Protestantism attempted to eradicate the popular perception of the priest as a magical resource, people continued to look upon Protestant ministers and pastors as having a talent for healing and dealing with witches and evil spirits, even if they were unable to conduct the rite of exorcism.

Across to Asia, and in China before the Revolution, the *sai kong* marketed themselves as Taoist priests and were popularly thought of as such. They operated from their own homes, with signboards advertising 'there is a Taoist altar here' or some such. They officiated in formal dress around their domestic altars furnished with images of the gods. They sold magical merchandise such as prayers, charms, images, and incantations. Through his knowledge and rituals, the *sai kong* could direct the power of gods and spirits to help his customers, and proved efficacious for exorcising evil spirits and healing spiritual illnesses. The magical reputations of the *sai kong*, like other magical practitioners around the globe, also rested to a degree on popular knowledge of their hereditary background.

How do you gain magical power and reputation if it is not based on formal or at least semi-formal religious authority and privilege? Gender is a fundamental issue here, for in some cultures women are excluded from such a communal role. In most African cultures, it would seem that witch-doctors were primarily men, for example. That is not to say that women were not thought to have magical abilities, but that in terms of beneficial magic and the protection of the community, they were often considered inferior to men because of issues of purity or physical strength. The hereditary principle in the transmission of magical powers can also inhibit access to magic. Yet in some cultures women were and are the paramount magicians. Among some Batak communities in Sumatra, female magicians were prized, and they played a dominant role as magical healers in some Native American tribes. Women practising Koranic magic might seem a contradiction in terms. But on a localized basis, literate women do practise Koranic magic, mostly for a female clientele, such as the female marabouts in the Sufi brotherhoods of Senegal.

In European history, at least from the medieval period onwards, we know of the importance of lay magicians that historians describe as cunning folk, though they have many regional and local names. One early 18th-century German pastor named Georg Zimmermann characterized them as 'hangmen, knackers, old women, gypsies, shepherds, herdsmen, Jews, peasants, tramps and mountebanks'. This was a jaundiced but not wholly inaccurate description. What defined cunning folk was not their social marginality, though, but the breadth of their magical services. They did not restrict themselves to simple healing or fortune telling, but offered to recover stolen property, procure love, draw up horoscopes, find treasure, provide herbal medicines, and, most important of all, deal with witches. Their practices were illegal under the raft of laws introduced across Europe during the 16th century against witchcraft and magic, but few were prosecuted because their beneficial services outweighed concerns over their ability to do harmful magic. Laws against fraudulent pretences and illegal medical practice likewise did little to undermine their role in the 18th and 19th centuries. They remained important figures in the social landscape of Europe into the 20th century.

The letters sent by clients to an English cunning man named William Brewer (1818–90) of Taunton, Somerset, give a flavour of their activities and how such people served as folk therapists. One young woman wrote,

> would you show me the man that will be my husband, or would you draw out my nativity for me. Sir, there is another young man that will not speak to me. He has walked with me twice and I have drank with him. Could you make him speak to me and be my husband if I wished?

Another asked,

> There is a person coming to the house that I live in to work. She is a great enemy of mine. She is coming on Wednesday. Could you manage to prevent her coming?

A woman inquired,

> Having heard of you by a friend I write to ask if you could tell me about my son. He is abroad. I am a widow and I feel very anxious about him.

Another widow wrote,

> Will you be kind enough to write and tell me if there is not something wrong with me and my cattle, for I get nothing but bad luck, for everything I take in hand goes wrong.

She clearly suspected witchcraft.

Cunning folk accrued their power in several ways. From the 16th century onwards, literacy was an important asset, and the possession of magic books key to generating a reputation in a largely illiterate society. Women had less access to an education and, until the 18th century, female literacy remained very low, particularly in Catholic countries. For many cunning women, then, reputation was based on their relations with supernatural beings, such as the spirits of the dead or the saints. The investigations of the Inquisition in early modern Sicily uncovered women who said they gained their beneficial powers from their frequent meetings with the fairies. These women, called the *donas de fuera* (ladies from outside), attracted the fairies because they had 'sweet blood'. Birthright was also important in marking out people as having magical authority. Being born with a caul was one sign, while being the seventh son of a seventh son conferred healing power. The *táltosok* of Hungary had an extra finger or were born with teeth.

In Islamic religion, two types of supernatural non-humans are officially recognized – angels and djinns. Djinns are distinct from the spirits of the dead and demons, and were created before humans existed. While angels are made of light, djinns were generated from smokeless fire. There are 'djinn Islam' that are benign and 'djinn kafir' which are evil, cause illnesses, possess people, and render men impotent. While confirming their existence, the Koran is clear that the djinn do not have predictive powers or the ability to discover hidden things. They tend to be found in impure places in and around the home, in bathrooms, graveyards, and rubbish heaps. They prefer the dark, and generally interact with the human world from dusk onwards. In many respects, they live everyday lives not dissimilar to humans, but they have extraordinary powers too, such as shape-shifting and super-human strength. Djinns cause harm but are also deemed an important source of counter-magic to heal and protect. King Solomon was fabled to owe his powers to his control of djinns. Modern Islamic magicians claim to seek out djinns in their twilight haunts, and through them can help their clients increase their salary, gain friendships, and provide numerous other services.

In some cultures, magicians only receive their powers after undergoing gruelling ritual initiations, usually under the mentorship of another magician. Prospective magicians amongst the Marind of New Guinea had to eat fried bananas for between five to seven days while an experienced magician created a potion including corpse juice. The novice had to drink this potion repeatedly while corpse juice was also dripped into his eyes and nose. Many such rituals are thought to enable the magician to communicate with the spirit world, and it is this relationship that provides them with their power. Such initiations are commonly associated with shamanism. In essence, shamanism, as an anthropological concept, concerns the mastering of trance states to mediate with the spirit world either by controlled possession or through magical flights into the world of spirits. The training process is illustrated well by the arduous path taken by the novice shamans of the Tamang of Nepal. The process is both didactic and ecstatic in nature. Initiates are identified by having had some mental crisis or revelatory spiritual experience. This may consist of visions or assaults by evil spirits. They begin their shamanic training by learning numerous myths and *mantra* (sounds, songs, or words that generate a spiritual transformation). Through these and instruction by other shamans, they learn to enter trance states. It takes years to master, and the money they earn afterwards is no great reward.

Magical traditions are not culturally exclusive. With respect to popular religion, just because priests and marabout said that the magic of other religions was as nothing compared to the power of the Bible or Koran, did not stop people from seeking the magic of the *other*. So in the records of the Spanish Inquisition, we find Christian Spaniards consulting those knowledgeable in Koranic magic. We also find examples from the Balkans. Official records from 18th-century Bosnia show that on a number of occasions, the local Ottoman Turkish authorities requested that Franciscan monks from the monastery of Fojnica use their prayers, talismans, and medicine to cure Muslim patients of possession by djinns or devils. There are numerous instances from the archives of Europe where Protestants sought out Catholic priests, requesting to be exorcised or to purchase blessed items.

Just like the ancient Persian *magoi*, over the centuries magical practitioners found themselves, by force, need, or professional ambition, offering their services in strange and foreign lands. Cultural as well as religious foreignness played an important part in shaping popular perceptions of magical ability. In Europe, the gypsies have long attracted reputations for magic, which they expertly exploited. In America and the Caribbean, syncretic magical traditions formed as different races and cultures were brought together. The conjure and hoodoo traditions of African Americans in the Southern states blended oral knowledge from Africa with Christian expressions of magic through the use of the Bible. Further additions to the mix were books of magic that derived from 18th-century Germany, and which spread from German settler communities to be adopted by African American conjure doctors. Terminology and practices also transferred the other way.

Material culture

The history of magic is not just a matter of oral and literary record. It often leaves material evidence. The horseshoe placed above the door is an obvious example. It is a physical reminder of the popular fear of witchcraft. Indeed, the literary archive provides us with only a partial understanding of the nature and range of magical practices in the past. Some traditions that have left an archaeological record were documented at the time of their use. Our knowledge of others can only by pieced together from interpreting the nature and location of deposited artefacts. The deliberate placement of shoes and clothing in chimneys and wall cavities, for instance, was evidently a widespread ritual building practice, but reference to it is absent from historical records. Likewise, recent finds of deliberately deposited horse skulls under early-modern limekilns, and ritual building marks, have left no archival record.

The material culture of magic has, unfortunately, received little attention from scholars compared to the literary archives. The main exception is the concept of the fetish. The term derives from the Latin *facticius* meaning 'artificial, made by art'. It first came into English usage in the 17th century via the Portuguese word *feitiço*. The Portuguese used it to describe the idols worshipped and magical objects worn or used by the populations of the West African coast, primarily Guinea, whom they encountered through trade. It was the French variation *fétiche* that, once anglicized, became widely adopted. Around the same time, in the 18th century, the French also adapted a West African word, *gris-gris*, from the Mende language, to describe specifically African charms and amulets.

While *gris-gris* would become part of the language of African American popular magic in the Southern states, it was 'fetish' that

10. Witch bottle found buried within the threshold of a property in King's Lynn, Norfolk, England, in 1905. The Bellarmine bottle is of late 17th century date and contained a cloth heart pierced with pins

became employed in a much broader intellectual and cultural context. In the minds of 19th-century social scientists, fetish came to be defined not just as an object but as a type of primitive religion that worshipped objects, either in an animistic sense or as a distinct magico-religious stage before the development of polytheism. Like other early social science terms, such as 'totem', it was also subsequently adopted by psychoanalysts, who used it to define a category of sexual pathology. More generally, fetishism was used as a derogatory, racist term for the magical or religious beliefs of African 'savages'. During the 20th century, these definitions were increasingly criticized, and they were largely dropped from scholarly anthropological discourse. Meanwhile, fetishes, which were collected by ethnographers and colonial officials and packed off to private collections, galleries, and museums, attracted increasing interest as art objects. Today, the meaning of 'fetish', and its cultural and colonial uses, has attracted renewed attention as a conceptual tool in interdisciplinary cultural theory.

'Fetish' as a term for a magical object was rarely applied to the material culture of European popular magic. It was racially defined. But a wealth of charms, amulets, and apotropaic, or protective, objects can be found in European museum collections alongside the 'exotic' ones that appealed to colonial collectors. There are items that protect the individual from harm when kept on the person or having them applied in some way by a magical healer. Across Europe, prehistoric stone arrowheads and axes were, for example, thought to have powers. Known as thunderstones in some cultures, they were treasured as a protection against lightning. In Scotland and Ireland, Bronze-Age flint arrowheads were thought to be fairy missiles used to harm cattle and people. Cunning folk, or fairy doctors, collected them to heal those who were 'elfshot'. The witch bottle is another object found in museum collections in England. It was a counter-witchcraft remedy based on sympathetic magic that seems to have developed in the 17th century. The victims of witchcraft, often on the advice of a cunning person, would pour their urine into a bottle along with some of their fingernails and hair. Sharp objects such as nails, pins, and thorns were added. The bottle represented the witch's bladder and, once boiled over a fire or buried under the hearth stone, the agitated contents would cause the witch excruciating pain. The practice found its way to America and became a part of African American magic, with conjure bottles containing harmful items taking the place of the more 'traditional' conjure bags in some areas. Practices aimed at protecting the home were also widespread. The secretion of personal items, horse skulls, dead cats, and other animals in wall and floor cavities and under thresholds is a ritual practice widely attested from excavations and house renovations in Europe and Australia, though few references to it are found in the literary record.

Chapter 6
Magic and the modern world

A century or more since the likes of Frazer, Tylor, and Weber expressed their groundbreaking theories, it is now clear that the age of science can accommodate an age of magic. Highly educated people have embraced magic as a challenge to scientific determinism, religious orthodoxy, and creative conformity. Modernity is not a synonym of rationality. In the last couple of decades, historians and cultural theorists have been exploring this re-enchantment of Western culture. They trace these issues back to the late 18th and early 19th centuries, at a time when the experience of life in industrializing European societies generated aesthetic reactions against the encroachment of mechanization, urbanization, and pollution. Progress was portrayed as a destructive force. The Romantic poets, essayists, and artists harked back to a halcyon classical pagan past set in a rural idyll, while in the present the last portal to an enchanted world was through emotion, memory, and imagination. One of the literary heirs to the Romantics, the Irish poet W. B. Yeats (1865–1939), expressed these sentiments in an essay on 'Magic' written in 1901:

> I have come to see or to imagine, in men and women, in houses, in handicrafts, in nearly all sights and sounds, a certain evil, a certain ugliness, that comes from the slow perishing through the centuries of a quality of mind that made this belief [magic] and its evidences common over the world.

Yeats was drawn to a new force that promised to re-enchant the world of the 19th-century middle classes: spiritualism. In mid-Victorian Britain, there was what some historians have described as a 'crisis of faith', a turning away from the sober, rationalist worship of the Church of England, a yearning for a more vital and spiritual connection. Modern spiritualism provided this. The movement began in America in 1848, when the adolescent Fox sisters of Hydesville, New York State, claimed that they could communicate with the spirits of the dead through knocks and raps. This age-old phenomenon, in the past blamed on witches or devils, was now reinterpreted and validated in the eyes of many: noisy hauntings moved from the realm of 'superstition' back to the heart of religion. For some, spiritualism was the recrudescence of diabolism; for some, profound confirmation of the Christian afterlife; and for others, a fraud to be debunked: magic, in multiple definitions, was back at the heart of religious and scientific investigation.

Spiritualism represented a 'crisis of evidence' as much as it highlighted a 'crisis of faith'. Its advent came a few years after the first telegraph messages had been sent. This scientific achievement made the notion of communicating with the spirit world all the more reasonable to many from both religious and scientific backgrounds. Consider Cromwell Varley (1828–83). A leading British expert in electronic engineering, who played a significant role in developing the trans-Atlantic telegraph system, Varley came to accept the existence of an electro-magnetic *spirit* telegraph. He did not come to this conclusion from blind faith but through scientific experimentation. While many spiritualist mediums were exposed as frauds, a few genuinely puzzled the scientific community. They raised questions about the limits of observable evidence and scientific authority.

Throughout the 18th and 19th centuries, there had been educated Europeans, mostly men, who had continued to explore intellectual forms of magic that had developed during the Renaissance and which, over the centuries, had disseminated via printed and manuscript books. While the Romantics thought about magic, these modern occultists rolled up their sleeves and did it. The social acceptance of spiritualism, the influence of the Theosophical movement, and the books of Eliphas Lévi, inspired a small group of British Freemasons to develop their own esoteric order, the Golden Dawn, of which W. B. Yeats was a member. Its founders created a series of rituals that combined the Judaeo-Christian magic formulated in medieval Europe with the magical traditions of the ancient Middle East and Asia, evidence for which had recently been translated into English. Other such small magical orders sprung up in Germany and France during the late 19th and early 20th centuries.

We find another expression of this educated embrace of the magical in the Surrealist movement of the early 20th century. As one of the pioneers of Surrealism, Max Ernst (1891–1976), wrote in 1942, magic was 'the means of approaching the unknown by other ways than those of science and religion'. Influenced by anthropological work on other far-flung cultures, drawing upon psychoanalysis, and intrigued by occultism and spiritualism, the Surrealists saw their art as acts of magical exploration. The Surrealist writer Julien Leiris (1901–90) mused in his diary for 1924, 'The work of art has no other end but the magical evocation of inner demons.' Their inspiration was given artistic representation in a pack of tarot cards designed by the poet André Breton and friends, in which the face cards were replaced with images of the likes of Paracelsus, Freud, the Marquis de Sade, Hegel, the medium Hélène Smith, Lewis Carroll's Alice, and the Mexican revolutionary Pancho Villa. Breton later went on to write *L'Art magique* (1957), a history of the relationship between art and magic from prehistory to the present.

The eclectic engagement with different magic traditions in Western Europe at the turn of the 20th century was an intellectual exercise in navigating the modern world through the magic of the

11. 'The Incantation' (1901), photograph by John Cimon Warburg (1867–1931). The photograph illustrates the interest in ritual magic in artistic circles at the time and the ability to manipulate photographs, which we see in much spiritualist photography

past. It was a self-conscious reflex born not of the need to control the environment, but of the desire to transform inner lives. The new magi were following their own journey to spiritual enlightenment. We can understand the movement from a historical social-cultural perspective, but need to be aware of its psychological meaning for individuals. The same goes, of course, for the resort to magic at any time in the past.

J. R. R. Tolkien's distinction between magic and enchantment neatly encapsulates these issues:

> Enchantment produces a Secondary World into which both designer and spectator can enter, to the satisfaction of their senses while they are inside; but in its purity it is artistic in desire and purpose. Magic produces, or pretends to produce, an alteration in the Primary World...it is not an art but a technique; its desire is power in this world, domination of things and wills.

These definitions are far from straightforward in a historic context, though. After all, the medieval scholars who worked magic were attempting enchantment in the sense that a 'Secondary World', the world of the occult, still existed in the 'Primary World'. So much remained unknown and unexplained. In this sense, the aim of magic was actually to disenchant the world. Furthermore, the desire for enchantment and magic were by no means mutually exclusive goals in a modern context. Aleister Crowley (1875–1947), a member of the Golden Dawn who went on to relish public notoriety as the 'Great Beast' and the 'wickedest man in the world', sought to achieve enchantment through magic, sex, and drugs, yet believed this journey had given him magical powers to control others.

Magic and technology

Moving from the abstract and intellectual to the practical and everyday, initial engagement with new technologies often inspires unscientific interpretations of how they function or can be manipulated. It is familiarity rather than scientific understanding that disenchants them. People can reject magical interpretations without adopting scientific explanation of technologies. How many people really understand how invisible waves transmitted through the air can be picked up by a simple bit of metal and turned into images and sound? Television, in other words. We just accept it as unmagical. Yet it still boggles many minds, and I can perfectly understand the actions of the elderly woman in early 20th-century England who, after having had electricity installed in her house, bunged up the plugholes when not in use to stop the electricity seeping out.

In 19th-century rural England, initial reactions to cameras and electricity generated magical interpretations of these strange new powers. In Somerset, having one's picture taken was described as being 'a tookt' and was akin to being 'wisht', or bewitched. The consequence was ill-fortune or early death. Likewise, when batteries began to appear in farms and workshops, accusations arose that their owners used 'electric power' to harm people in a fashion akin to witchcraft. Similar initial responses to the same technological advances can be found in cultures around the globe.

In the late 19th century, European explorers and missionaries presented their cameras as magical devices in order to establish their superiority or to obtain cultural access. The Scottish traveller Joseph Thomson adopted the persona of an *mganga*, or healer, in East Africa, telling the Masai that his photographs of their warriors would magically enhance their prowess in battle. Decades later, after the camera had been disenchanted, photographs were nevertheless co-opted into popular magic. In 1950s western Kenya, witch doctors developed cursing rituals whereby the photograph of an intended victim would bleed on being cut if the curse had been successful. For this reason, many people were reluctant to have their picture taken. A Christian fundamentalist group hit back by promoting the notion that having one's picture taken with the Bible would counteract any such sorcery. Photographs were also adopted in similar sympathetic magic practices in 19th- and early 20th-century America. Folklore collectors working in ethnic German and African American communities found photographs being used in the service of older forms of sympathetic magic. Bury the picture of your enemy face down and, as it fades, so too will your enemy's life. Likewise, the picture could be burned while muttering a charm, or a nail driven through it, or a coffin drawn on the back and the photo placed upside down to achieve the same ends.

Neither is technology immune from magical interference. Across the globe today, talismans are placed in cars to protect them as much as the occupants. Ethnographers working in the French Bocage during the 1970s and 1980s found that car accidents or breakdowns could be interpreted in terms of witchcraft. This notion is merely a technological updating of the frequent accusations in earlier European sources that witches caused cart wheels to break or wagons to get stuck in the mud. In parts of Africa, the introduction of tractors added a new dimension to agricultural witchcraft disputes. A study of road travel in Ghana found that the wrecks of cars and lorries at accident blackspots on otherwise good, new road surfaces attracted suspicions of witchcraft.

The mobile phone is the most recent technology to transform everyday African social relations. While the technology was not seen as magical, it was initially believed by some that it could be used as a vehicle for magical harm. In Nigeria in 2004, the recent mass ownership of mobile phones led to a public scare as rumours spread quickly across the country that anyone who answered calls from specific malign numbers would be struck mad or drop down dead. A surge of text messages hit the network as people contacted friends and family warning them of the numbers, some of which were printed in the newspapers. The concerns soon died down, of course. The scare is reminiscent of the backward masking Satanic scare in America during the early 1980s when heavy metal records were thought to contain Satanic messages that could only be heard by playing the record backwards. Claims were made that these could subliminally influence people to commit suicide or worship Satan. The scare was stoked by Christian fundamentalists, whose influence had grown hugely thanks to the recent explosion of cable television channels. Staying with the USA, the development of mobile phone 'apps' has led to entrepreneurs peddling spells and charms via this new medium.

Advertising lies at the nexus of art, technology, and commerce in the 20th century, and so it is not surprising that the language of enchantment and magic has been applied to its practitioners and power. Diet products that promise amazing results, deodorants that attract beautiful women, perfumes that entice men, shampoos that sell on the basis of pseudo-scientific mumbo-jumbo; the choice of words used to sell them is more important than their chemical contents. Advertising adds value to a product, transforms it, through the power of language and wish-fulfilment. Most important of all, it promises control over one's destiny just like magic – if you accept its blandishments, and millions do. If we did not still live in a magical world, the advertising industry would not exist as we know it.

The child within

We all have our magic moments. Have you never urged your car to go faster as it struggles up a slope? Made a wish? Believed that an event was more than coincidence? A desire for something to happen – 'I hope she loses her job' – may be expressed rationally, but if it comes true, the interpretation may turn magical. These are phenomena of our waking hours. In our dreams, our minds lead us into magical worlds and activities. We can fly. Our thoughts can change the dream world around us. The clinical condition known as sleep paralysis, which has been recorded in cultures across the world and in the historical record, can generate what seem like very real nocturnal assaults by supernatural entities. The 'victim' experiences temporary paralysis, auditory and visual hallucinations, and the physical sensation of a heavy weight upon the chest or throat. This has given rise to many testimonies of assault by witches, demons, ghosts, and aliens.

Even if some people reading this have never had such impulses or experiences, then it is certain that they had some magical moments when they were very young. As was noted in a previous chapter, psychologists have long been interested in the 'magical thinking' of children. A working definition proposed by the American Psychiatric Association states that it applies to someone who 'believes that his or her thoughts, words, or actions might, or will in some manner cause or prevent a specific outcome in some way that defies the normal laws of cause and effect'. Freud had equated childhood magical thinking with that of primitive societies and neurotics, seeing it as a survival of a primitive evolutionary stage. But it was pioneering developmental psychologist Jean Piaget who, in the 1920s, first began extensive empirical studies of childhood thought processes. In his early work, Piaget concluded that magical thinking derived from children's inability to differentiate between the mental and the physical.

It is between the ages of six and nine that most children are thought to abandon magical thinking as a conviction. But numerous recent studies suggest that children as young as three can have a quite sophisticated 'rational' sense of physical causality and yet still exhibit magical thinking. The developmental psychologist Eugene Subbotsky conducted an experiment whereby he presented four-year-olds with a 'magic' table that resembled one that he had described to them in a story about a girl who had just such a magic table that could turn toy animals into real ones. Asked if they thought such a thing could happen, only a few children said 'yes'. But when a toy lion was placed on the magic table and moved with magnets, most showed signs of fear that the lion had become real, or they waved a magic wand over it that the psychologists had supplied them with to stop it moving. So the children verbally expressed a rational opinion but, when faced with an apparent magical action, they reacted in a magical way.

Magical thinking has also been explored in terms of children's *explanations* as well as desires – how they understand life and death, for example. Consider one five-year-old's explanation for what happens when people die: 'They go back into their Mummy's tummy and become a teeny-weeny baby again.' Sounds like reincarnation. Early childhood reasoning throws up other analogies with the fundamentals of religion. Children's intuitive assumption that inanimate objects have sentience is essentially an animistic belief.

Far from espousing a rational view of the world, parents from cultures across the globe actively encourage magical thinking in pre-school children. They provide magical explanations to satisfy children in their early stages of inquisitiveness about why things work or happen. Children's books feed magical fantasies, and early-years children's television presents magical worlds that bear little relationship to the real world. Why do we nourish magical thinking? What are the lasting consequences? The question has repeatedly been asked, is Harry Potter harmful? As one might expect, the answers are varied, inconclusive, and open to multiple interpretations. Nothing is simple when it comes to understanding human cognitive development, with opinion divided at the fundamental level of the influence of nature and nurture. From a positive perspective, it has been suggested that children can absorb from fairy tales and fantasies valuable lessons in identifying socially valued attributes such as charity, friendship, and trust. The exploration of magical worlds also enables children to work out the boundaries between reality and fantasy as their critical perception develops. Magical thinking might also stimulate abstract and theoretical interpretations that have value in the development of our intellectual and creative faculties.

Magical belief provides children with essential coping strategies for dealing with stress and tragedy that they are otherwise emotionally unequipped to deal with.

Back in the 17th and 18th centuries, educationalists repeatedly claimed that telling young children folktales and accounts of ghosts, witches, and fairies could cause lasting damage. Boys would grow into timid and depressive men, and girls into foolish and superstitious women. There is little evidence in the modern literature on developmental psychology to support this notion of life-long influence, but claims have been made for a link between magical thinking in children and their exhibition of obsessive-compulsive behaviour. A recent study of 102 school children did not support this, however, but still revealed a correlation with more general anxiety symptoms.

In much developmental psychology, magic is still defined as belonging to the other, but this time the other is our childhood. We think in terms of 'losing' our childhood, and with it our magical selves, as we enter adulthood. Modern Western society likes to maintain this 'otherness'. The expression of magical thinking in adulthood is considered by many as abnormal, and is open to definition in terms of anxiety, neurosis, and psychosis. But, as we have already seen, the adult belief in magic cannot be reduced to pathological explanations.

A universal experience?

So we have all thought magically at some point. How we deal with it in adulthood is influenced by history, society, culture, education, and personal experience. In most societies, organized religion provides a culturally acceptable framework for rationalizing the continuance of magical thinking. This has been described as 'institutionalized magical belief'. Mechanistic forms of worship such as prayer and ritual can be perceived as either magical or religious depending on who performs it and in what context.

Think back to the discussion of popular religion in the Introduction. Believing that a god or gods can influence earthly affairs or determine our existence after death is essentially magical thinking as understood in developmental psychology.

Émile Durkheim once wrote that 'there is something eternal in religion which is destined to survive all the particular symbols in which religious thought has successively enveloped itself'. 'Religion' could be swapped with 'magic' and the statement would still hold. Trying to identify what that 'something' is has led more recent scholars to suggest that as an experience magic and religion, past and present, are based on universal cognitive processes. Cognition refers to the way in which knowledge is acquired, how it is organized in the mind, and then employed both consciously and unconsciously. One example of how this can applied is the suggestion that the magic impulse derives from early human development of tool use. According to this idea, brain function used in language did not develop for communication but for using things. If words developed from 'thing using', then this would help to explain the human urge to employ words to make things happen.

Less speculative is the work on contagious magic and cognition. Modern adults display a range of secular activities that reflect notions of contagion. Place a can of drink near some excrement, and most people would be reluctant to drink it if offered, even if it is unopened and subsequently sterilized. Many people feel disgust at the idea of wearing second-hand clothes. Such negative cognitive responses perhaps developed because, although irrational, they serve an advantageous function in avoiding real sources of contagion. We also exhibit 'positive' contagious impulses such as celebrity memento hunting, feeling a lasting emotional link with a star through the possession of something tangible. Consider the desire of fans to touch pop idols. In other cultures, contagion cognition also continues to be expressed in religious and secular ways.

If we accept that magical thinking and behaviour are universal cognitive traits, then they can presumably help us to explain aspects of magic in historical contexts because we share the same mental and physical experiences today. A few attempts have been made to explore this. Using orthodox and apocryphal early Christian writings and Greek magical papyri as sources, a cognitive theory of magic has been proposed that is based on three interrelated factors. First, there is the consumption of stories about magic and miracles, which provide examples, explanations, and inspiration. Second, beliefs that ensure that magic makes sense. Third, conditioned behaviour such as repetitive actions, unconscious manipulations, and the impulses described above. A more eclectic approach has been adopted in a recent book that seeks, as its title states, to understand *The Realities of Witchcraft and Popular Magic in Early Modern Europe*. In this, the author uses neuroscience and psychology to explore the role of dreams, trances, intoxication, and other forms of altered perception, in generating 'real' experiences that confirmed beliefs regarding the effects of magical practices. An awareness of the science of cognition is clearly important for understanding the meaning of magic historically, but of course we are still faced with the problem of our distance from the past, and the selective evidence that has come down to us. How many people, for example, had what we might label magical experiences in a modern cognitive sense, but which they did not interpret magically? Historians of magic and witchcraft work with sources that provide glimpses into individual neuro-psychological experiences, but rarely confirm universal cognitive explanations. That does not mean they do not exist.

Back to the present and what 'magical experience' means in the contemporary world. One modern British anthropologist has analysed how her own experience of magic is not necessarily supernatural or mystical, nor an aspect of modern or post-modern crisis, but rather 'an *emotional* relationship with place through notions of ancestors, folk beliefs and myths'. Nature is at the heart of this sense of magic. This could be interpreted as a product of self-reflexive, Western intellectual reasoning. But similar ideas of *magical consciousness* have been expressed with regard to the relationship between magicians and their clients in the Indian city of Banaras: 'The magician is the man or woman who creates the context in which minds enter a relationship, and this is often experiences as an "occult" event. And although the experience is in fact extraordinary, it is completely natural.' This conclusion could also be dismissed as an expression of Western intellectual reasoning, but such studies help break down the cultural and emotional barriers between observer and participant, and provide clues to unlocking what magic means when it is enacted. All too often a sense of magic is lost in the process of studying magic, but this need not be the case.

Final thoughts

Magic cannot be consigned to the past, dismissed as the product of ignorance, or ranked as an evolutionary stage of human thought – at least not in cultural terms. As this *Very Short Introduction* demonstrates, since it was first expressed conceptually back in antiquity, it has accrued a range of meanings that ensure it retains its relevance in every society today. Magic is far more than a venerable collection of practices. We need to understand it as a language, a theory, a belief, an action, a creative expression, an experience, and a cognitive tool. It is integral to religion and yet can be independent of it. An atheist can believe in magic. Yes, science has undermined the basis of magic as an explanation for natural processes. It has rendered magic's role in medicine largely redundant by providing clearly superior results – for those of us who can profit from them. But while science gives us explanations and solutions, it also provides us with a choice. It can help explain magic but cannot explain it away – magic is always an alternative. In its broadest sense, magic is a part of the human condition. To believe magic will eventually disappear is mere wishful thinking.

References

Introduction

On ancient terminology regarding magic, see Matthew W. Dickie, *Magic and Magicians in the Greco-Roman World* (London, 2001), chapter 1; Stephen Charles Haar, *Simon Magus: The First Gnostic?* (Berlin, 2003), pp. 33–70; J. N. Bremmer, 'The Birth of the Term "Magic"', *Zeitschrift für Papyrologie und Epigraphik*, 129 (1999): 1–12; Albert de Jong, *Traditions of the Magi* (Leiden, 1997).

On the biblical magi, see M. A. Powell, 'The Magi as Wise Men: Re-Examining a Basic Supposition', *New Testament Studies*, 46, 1 (2000): 1–20; Richard C. Trexler, *The Journey of the Magi: Meanings in History of a Christian Story* (Princeton, 1997); Jerry Vardaman and Edwin M. Yamauchi (eds.), *Chronos, Kairos, Christos: Nativity and Chronological Studies Presented to Jack Finegan* (Winona Lake, 1989).

David E. Aune, 'Magic in Early Christianity', in Hildegard Temporini and Wolfgang Haase (eds.), *Aufstieg und Niedergang der Römischen Welt II* (Berlin, 1980), pp. 1470–1557.

Owen Davies, *A Very Short Introduction to Paganism* (Oxford, 2011).

On the Jewish blood libel, see R. Po-chia Hsia, *The Myth of Ritual Murder: Jews and Magic in Reformation Germany* (New Haven, 1988); Francesca Matteoni, 'The Jew, the Blood and the Body in Late Medieval and Early Modern Europe', *Folklore*, 119, 2 (2008): 182–200.

Weber quote from Max Weber, *Economy and Society: An Outline of Interpretive Sociology* (Berkeley, 1978), vol. 2, p. 467.

Zwemer quote from Samuel Marinus Zwemer, *The Influence of Animism in Islam* (New York, 1920), p. 163.

Helen L. Parish, *Monks, Miracles and Magic: Reformation Representations of the Medieval Church* (Abingdon, 2005).

On attitudes towards Sufism, see Eva Evers Rosander and David Westerlund (eds.), *African Islam and Islam in Africa: Encounters between Sufis and Islamists* (London, 1997); Scott Alan Kugle, *Sufis and Saints' Bodies: Mysticism, Corporeality, and Sacred Power in Islam* (Chapel Hill, 2007); Martin van Bruinessen, 'Sufism, "Popular" Islam and the Encounter with Modernity', in Muhammad Khalid Masud, Armando Salvatore, and Martin van Bruinessen (eds.), *Islam and Modernity: Key Issues and Debates* (Edinburgh, 2009), chapter 5.

On the Brahmins and magic, see Gyan Prakash, 'The Colonial Genealogy of Society: Community and Political Modernity in India', in Patrick Joyce (ed.), *The Social in Question: New Bearings in History and the Social Sciences* (London, 2002), pp. 81–97; Ruth S. Freed and Stanley A. Freed, 'Unity in Diversity in the Celebration of Cattle-Curing Rites in a North Indian Village: A Study in the Resolution of Conflict', *American Anthropologist*, N.S. 68, 3 (1966): 673–92.

On *shirk* and magic in Islam, see Kathleen M. O'Connor, 'Idolatry', in Juan Eduardo Campo (ed.), *Encyclopedia of Islam* (New York, 2009), pp. 343–4; Ahmad Dallal, 'The Origins and Objectives of Islamic Revivalist Thought, 1750–1850', *Journal of the American Oriental Society*, 113, 3 (1993): 341–59; Alexander Rodrigues, 'Wahhabism and "the Peoples' Islam" in the Arabian Peninsula', in Nur Kirabaev and Yuriy Pochta (eds.), *Values in Islamic Culture and the Experience of History* (Washington, 2002), chapter 10.

Abduh quote cited in J. J. G. Jansen, *The Interpretation of the Koran in Modern Egypt* (Leiden, 1974), p. 31.

T. Jeremy Gunn, 'Shaping an Islamic Identity: Religion, Islamism, and the State in Central Asia', *Sociology of Religion*, 64, 3 (2003): 389–410.

Quote on black magic in Malaysia cited in Sylva Frisk, *Submitting to God: Women and Islam in Urban Malaysia* (Seattle, 2009), p. 103.

On syncretic religions in the Caribbean, see, for example, Margarite Fernández Olmos and Lizabeth Paravisini-Gebert, *Creoloe Religions of the Caribbean: An Introduction from Vodou and Santería to Obeah and Espiritismo* (New York, 2003).

Islam in Africa quote from Timothy Insoll, *The Archaeology of Islam in Sub-Saharan Africa* (Cambridge, 2003), p. 34.

Raquel Romberg, *Witchcraft and Welfare: Spiritual Capital and the Business of Magic in Modern Puerto Rico* (Austin, 2003).

Chapter 1

For a brief overview of evolutionary theories of religion and magic, see Graham Cunningham, *Religion and Magic: Approaches and Theories* (Edinburgh, 1999). More detailed studies include Garry Trompf, *In Search of Origins* (New Delhi, 1990); Stanley J. Tambiah, *Magic, Science, Religion, and the Scope of Rationality* (Cambridge, 1990); Dorothy Hammond, 'Magic: A Problem in Semantics', *American Anthropologist* N.S. 72, 6 (1970): 1349–56; Randall Styers, *Making Magic: Religion, Magic, and Science in the Modern World* (Oxford, 2004); Daniel O'Keefe, *Stolen Lightning: The Social Theory of Magic* (Oxford, 1982).

Jesper Sørensen, *A Cognitive Theory of Magic* (Lanham, 2007); George Stocking, *After Tylor: British Social Anthropology 1888–1951* (London, 1999); Jacob Neusner, Ernest S. Frerichs, and Paul Virgil McCracken Flesher (eds.), *Religion, Science, and Magic: In Concert and in Conflict* (Oxford, 1989).

On Wittgenstein, see, for example, Brian R. Clack, *Wittgenstein, Frazer and Religion*; D. Z. Phillips, 'Wittgenstein, Wittgensteinianism, and Magic: A Philosophical Tragedy?', *Religious Studies*, 39 (2003): 185–201; Thomas de Zengotita, 'On Wittgenstein's *Remarks on Frazer's Golden Bough*', *Cultural Anthropology*, 4, 4 (1989): 390–8.

Stanley J. Tambiah, *Culture, Thought and Social Action: An Anthropological Perspective* (Cambridge, 1985).

Gunter Senft, 'Bronisław Kasper Malinowski', in Gunter Senft, Jan-Ola Östman, and Jef Verschueren (eds.), *Culture and Language Use* (Amsterdam, 2009), pp. 217–21.

M. G. Marwick, 'The Study of Witchcraft', in A. L. Epstein (ed.), *The Craft of Anthropology* (Oxford, 1967), pp. 235–5; Peter Pels, 'The Magic of Africa: Reflections on a Western Commonplace', *African Studies Review*, 41, 3 (1998): 193–209; Elias K. Bongmba, 'Evans-Pritchard and the Theoretical Demise of the Concept of Magic', in James Kiernan (ed.), *The Power of the Occult in Modern Africa* (Berlin, 2006), pp. 19–45.

Murray Wax and Rosalie Wax, 'The Notion of Magic', *Current Anthropology*, 4, 5 (1963): 495–518.

Robert Redfield, 'The Primitive World View', *Proceedings of the American Philosophical Society*, 96 (1952): 30–6; Michael Kearney, 'World View Theory and Study', *Annual Review of Anthropology*, 4 (1975): 247–70.
George M. Foster, 'Peasant Society and the Image of Limited Good', *American Anthropologist*, 67 (1965): 293–315. See also Foster, 'A Second Look at Limited Good', *Anthropological Quarterly*, 45 (1972): 57–64.
John Lindow, 'Swedish Legends of Buried Treasure', *Journal of American Folklore*, 95 (1982): 257–79.
Laura Stark-Arola, *Magic, Body and Social Order: The Construction of Gender Through Women's Private Rituals in Traditional Finland* (Helsinki, 1998), pp. 116–17.
Anthony H. Galt, 'Magical Misfortune in Locorotondo', *American Ethnologist*, 18, 4 (1991): 735–50.
On the anthropology of traditional witchcraft in modern Europe, see Willem de Blécourt, 'The Witch, Her Victim, the Unwitcher and the Researcher: The Continued Presence of Traditional Witchcraft', in Willem de Blécourt, Ronald Hutton, and Jean Sybil de la Fontaine, *Witchcraft and Magic in Europe: The Twentieth Century* (London, 1999), pp. 141–220; Richard Jenkins, 'Continuity and Change: Social Science Perspectives on European Witchcraft', in Jonathan Barry and Owen Davies (eds.), *Witchcraft Historiography* (Basingstoke, 2007), pp. 203–25.
Julian Pitt-Rivers, *The People of the Sierra* (London, 1954).
Richard Blum and Eva Blum, *Healing in Rural Greece* (Stanford, 1965); *The Dangerous Hour: The Lore and Culture of Crisis and Mystery in Rural Greece* (New York, 1970).
On De Martino, see George R. Saunders, '"Critical Ethnocentrism" and the Ethnology of Ernesto De Martino', *American Anthropologist*, N.S. 95, 4 (1993): 875–93; Roberto Cipriani, *Sociology of Religion: An Historical Introduction*, tr. Laura Ferrarotti (New York, 2000), pp. 135–7.
Jeanne Favret-Saada, *Les mots, la mort, les sorts* (Paris, 1977).
Owen Davies, 'Witchcraft Accusations in France, 1850–1990', in Willem de Blécourt and Owen Davis (eds.), *Witchcraft Continued: Popular Magic in Modern Europe* (Manchester, 2004), chapter 6.
Inge Schöck, *Hexenglaube in der Gegenwart* (Tübingen, 1978).
Hans Sebald, *Witchcraft: The Heritage of a Heresy* (New York, 1978); Hans Sebald, 'The Demise of a Folk Magic', *Anthropological Quarterly*, 53 (1980): 173–87.

Chapter 2

On the *Cheiromecta*, see Matthew W. Dickie, *Magic and Magicians in the Greco-Roman World* (London, 2001), pp. 119–23.

On the early histories of magic, see Jan N. Bremmer, 'Magic in the Apocryphal Acts of the Apostles', in Jan N. Bremmer and Jan R. Veenstra (eds.), *The Metamorphosis of Magic from Late Antiquity to the Early Modern Period* (Leuven, 2002), p. 53; Owen Davies, *Grimoires: A History of Magic Books* (Oxford, 2009), pp. 7–10; Lynn Thorndike, *A History of Magic and Experimental Science* (New York, 1923), vol. 1, pp. 414–15, 558–60; Gideon Bohak, *Ancient Jewish Magic: A History* (Cambridge, 2008), p. 81; Ayse Tuzlak, 'The Magician and the Heretic: The Case of Simon Magus', in Paul Allan Mirecki and Marvin W. Meyer (eds.), *Magic and Ritual in the Ancient World* (Leiden, 2002), pp. 416–26.

Simon Ravensberg quote in Peter Maxwell-Stuart, 'The Contemporary Historical Debate, 1400–1750', in Jonathan Barry and Owen Davies (eds.), *Witchcraft Historiography* (Basingstoke, 2007), p. 13.

Gabriel Naudé, *The History of Magick* (London, 1657). See Maryanne Cline Horowitz, 'Gabriel Naudé's Apology for Great Men Suspected of Magic: Variations in Editions from 1625–1715', in John Christian Laursen (ed.), *Histories of Heresy in Early Modern Europe* (Basingstoke, 2002), pp. 61–77; Lauren Kassell, '"All was this land full fill'd of faerie", or Magic and the Past in Early Modern England', *Journal of the History of Ideas*, 67, 1 (2006): 107–22.

Naudé quote from Gabriel Naudé, *The History of Magick*, p. 65.

Vaughan quotes from Thomas Vaughan, *Magia Adamica: or the Antiquitie of Magic* (London, 1650), p. C2v, p. 7.

Howitt quote from William Howitt, *The History of the Supernatural* (London, 1863), vol. 1, p. 75.

Joseph Ennemoser, *The History of Magic* (London, 1854), vol. 1, pp. 187, 189.

Lévi quote from Éliphas Lévi, *The History of Magic*, tr. A. E. Waite (London, 1913), p. 72.

On the Occult Revival, see, most recently, Alison Butler, *Victorian Occultism and the Making of Modern Magic: Invoking Tradition* (Basingstoke, 2011).

Art Magic: Or Mundane, Sub Mundane, and Super Mundane Spiritism (New York, 1876), p. 175.

Isaac Schapera, *The Khoisan Peoples of South America* (London, 1930), pp. 168, 198.

On magic and paganism, see Owen Davies, *A Very Short Introduction to Paganism* (Oxford, 2011).

Lynn Thorndike, *A History of Magic and Experimental Science* (New York, 1923), vol. 1, p. 2. See Karen Jolly, 'Medieval Magic: Definitions, Beliefs, Practices', in Karen Jolly, Catharina Raudvere, and Edward Peters (eds.), *Witchcraft and Magic in Europe: The Middle Ages* (London, 2001); Michael D. Bailey, *Magic and Superstition in Europe: A Concise History from Antiquity to the Present* (Lanham, 2007), chapters 3 and 4; Joel Kaye, 'Law, Magic, and Science: Constructing a Border between Licit and Illicit Knowledge in the Writings of Nicole Oresme', in Ruth Mazo Karras, E. Ann Matter, and Joel Kaye (eds.), *Law and the Illicit in Medieval Europe* (Philadelphia, 2008), chapter 16.

Richard Kieckhefer, *Magic in the Middle Ages* (Cambridge, 1989), p. 1. On the science/magic debate, see also Randall Styers, 'The "Magic" of "Science": The Labelling of Ideas', in Glenn Hudak and Paul Kihn (eds.), *Labelling: Pedagogy and Politics* (London, 2001), chapter 15.

On the debate over magic and the scientific revolution, see Frances Yates, *Giordano Bruno and the Hermetic Tradition* (Cambridge, 1964); Brian Vickers (ed.), *Occult and Scientific Mentalities in the Renaissance* (Cambridge, 1984); Steven Shapin, *The Scientific Revolution* (Chicago, 1996); John Henry, *The Scientific Revolution and the Origins of Modern Science* (Basingstoke, 2008), chapter 4.

John Wilkins, *Mathematicall Magick, Or, The Wonders that May be Performed by Mechanicall Geometry* (London, 1648), preface. See J. Peter Zetterberg, 'The Mistaking of "the Mathematicks" for Magic in Tudor and Stuart England', *Sixteenth Century Journal*, 11, 1 (1980): 83–97.

Stuart Clark, *Thinking with Demons* (Oxford, 1997); James Sharpe, *Instruments of Darkness: Witchcraft in England 1550–1750* (London, 1996), chapter 11; Malcolm Gaskill, *A Very Short Introduction to Witchcraft* (Oxford, 2010), chapter 4.

Gilbert G. Germain, *A Discourse on Disenchantment: Reflections on Politics and Technology* (Albany, 1993).

Thomas's work is rich in ideas beyond the disenchantment thesis. For critical assessments of *Religion and the Decline of Magic*, see Jonathan Barry, 'Keith Thomas and the Problem of Witchcraft', in Jonathan Barry, Marianne Hester, and Gareth Roberts (eds.), *Witchcraft in Early Modern Europe: Studies in Popular Culture and Belief* (Cambridge, 1996), pp. 1–46; Alan Macfarlane, 'Civility and the Decline of Magic', in Paul Slack, Peter Burke, and Brian Harrison (eds.), *Civil Histories: Essays Presented to Sir Keith Thomas* (Oxford, 2000), chapter 8.

R. W. Scribner, 'The Reformation, Popular Magic, and the "Disenchantment of the World"', *Journal of Interdisciplinary History*, 23, 3 (1993): 475–94; Alexandra Walsham, 'The Reformation and "The Disenchantment of the World Reassessed"', *The Historical Journal*, 51, 2 (2008): 497–528; Michael D. Bailey, 'The Disenchantment of Magic: Spells, Charms, and Superstition in Early European Witchcraft Literature', *American Historical Review*, 3, 2 (2006): 383–404; Philip M. Soergel, 'Miracle, Magic, and Disenchantment in Early Modern Germany', in Peter Schäfer and Hans Gerhard Kippenberg (eds.), *Envisioning Magic* (Leiden, 1997), pp. 215–35; Edward Bever, 'Witchcraft Prosecutions and the Decline of Magic', *Journal of Interdisciplinary History*, 40, 2 (2009): 263–93; Karl Bell, 'Breaking Modernity's Spell – Magic and Modern History', *Cultural and Social History*, 4, 1 (2007): 115–23.

Chapter 3

Derek Collins, *Magic in the Ancient Greek World* (Oxford, 2008), pp. 33–54.

F. Gerald Downing, 'Magic and Scepticism in and around the First Christian Century', in Todd Klutz (ed.), *Magic in the Biblical World: From the Rod of Aaron to the Ring of Solomon* (London, 2003), pp. 86–100.

Ibn Khaldūn quote in Mushegh Asatrian, 'Ibn Khaldūn on Magic and the Occult', *Iran and the Caucasus*, 7, 1–2 (2003): 99.

Scot quote from Reginald Scot, *The Discoverie of Witchcraft* (London, [1584] 1930), p. 182.

Ady quotes from Thomas Ady, *A Candle in the Dark Shewing the Divine Cause of the Distractions of the Whole Nation of England and of the Christian World* (London, 1655), pp. 36, 29.

On ventriloquism, see Steven Connor, *Dumbstruck: A Cultural History of Ventriloquism* (Oxford, 2000); Owen Davies, *The Haunted: A Social History of Ghosts* (Basingstoke, 2007), pp. 154–7.

Benjamin G. Kohl and H. C. Erik Midelfort, *On Witchcraft: An Abridged Translation of Johann Weyer's De præstigiis dæmonum* (Asheville, 1998), p. 64.

Porta quote from *Natural magick by John Baptista Porta, a Neapolitane* (London, 1658), p. 358.

On optical magic, see Stuart Clark, *Vanities of the Eye: Vision in Early Modern European Culture* (Oxford, 2007); Davies, *The Haunted*, chapter 7.

On Houdin, see Graham Jones, 'Modern Magic and the War on Miracles in French Colonial Culture', *Comparative Studies in Society and History*, 52 (2010): 67.

On India, see Peter Lamont, *The Rise of the Indian Rope Trick: The Biography of a Legend* (London, 2005); Lee Siegel, *Net of Magic: Wonders and Deceptions in India* (Chicago, 1991).

Montaigne quoted in Jonathan L. Pearl, 'Montaigne, Michel de', in Richard M. Golden (ed.), *Encyclopedia of Witchcraft: The Western Tradition* (Santa Barbara, 2006), vol. 3, p. 780.

Weyer quote from *On Witchcraft*, p. 100.

On Charcot and witchcraft, see H. C. Erik Midelfort, 'Charcot, Freud, and the Demons', in Kathryn A. Edwards (ed.), *Werewolves, Witches, and Wandering Spirits* (Kirksville, 2002), pp. 199–217; David Lederer, *Madness, Religion and the State in Early Modern Europe: A Bavarian Beacon* (Cambridge, 2006), chapter 7; Roy Porter, 'Witchcraft and Magic in Enlightenment, Romantic and Liberal Thought', in Marijke Gijswijt-Hofstra, Brian P. Levack, and Roy Porter (eds.), *Witchcraft and Magic in Europe: The Eighteenth and Nineteenth Centuries* (London, 1999), pp. 266–73.

On Weyer and the psychiatric profession, see Peter Elmer, 'Science, Medicine and Witchcraft', in Jonathan Barry and Owen Davies (eds.), *Witchcraft Historiography* (Basingstoke, 2007), pp. 35–9.

For overviews of Freud and magic, see Jesper Sørensen, *A Cognitive Theory of Magic*, pp. 27–8; Graham Cunningham, *Religion and Magic: Approaches and Theories* (Edinburgh, 1999), pp. 25–8; Dave Green, '*Wishful Thinking*? Notes towards a Psychoanalytic Sociology of Pagan Magic', *Journal for the Academic Study of Magic*, 2 (2004): 48–79.

Freud's description of Charcot quoted in Christopher G. Goetz, Michel Bonduelle, and Toby Gelfand, *Charcot: Constructing Neurology* (Oxford, 1995), p. 269.

Freud quotes from Sigmund Freud, *Totem and Taboo* (London, 1950), pp. 78, 83.

Géza Róheim, *Magic and Schizophrenia* (New York, 1955), p. 3.

On Malinowski and Freud, see Ivan Strenski, *Thinking About Religion: An Historical Introduction to Theories of Religion* (Oxford, 2006), chapter 10.

Jean Piaget, *The Child's Conception of Physical Causality* (London, 1930).

Gustav Jahoda, *The Psychology of Superstition* (London, 1969), p. 7.

Richard Wiseman and Caroline Watt, 'Measuring Superstitious Belief: Why Lucky Charms Matter', *Personality and Individual Differences*, 37 (2004): 1533–41.

Stuart A. Vyse, *Believing in Magic: The Psychology of Superstition* (Oxford, 1997), pp. 177–80.

Harvey J. Irwin, *The Psychology of Paranormal Belief: A Researcher's Handbook* (Hatfield, 2009); Leonard Zusne and Warren H. Jones, *Anomalistic Psychology: A Study of Magical Thinking* (Hillsdale, 1989), p. 13.

Jerome J. Tobacyk, 'A Revised Paranormal Belief Scale', *International Journal of Transpersonal Studies*, 23 (2004); Wai-Cheong Carl Tam and Yung-Jong Shiah, 'Paranormal Belief, Religiosity and Cognitive Complexity', *The Parapsychological Assocation Convention* (2004).

Chapter 4

Islamic guideline quoted in Gerda Sengers, *Women and Demons: Cult Healing in Islamic Egypt* (Boston, 2003), p. 45.

Wahid Ibn Abdessalam Bali, *Sword Against Black Magic and Evil Magicians*, tr. Chafik Abdelghani (London, 2004). For discussion on Bali's work, see Remke Kruk, 'Harry Potter in the Gulf: Contemporary Islam and the Occult', *British Journal of Middle Eastern Studies*, 31, 1 (2005): 47–73.

Cyril Elgood, 'Tibb-ul-Nabbi or Medicine of the Prophet', *Osiris*, 14 (1962): 157.

Abdullahi Osman El-Tom, 'Drinking the Koran: The Meaning of Koranic Verses in Berti Erasure', *Africa*, 55, 4 (1985): 423.

Bess Allen Donaldson, 'The Koran as Magic', *The Moslem World*, 27 (1937) pp. 254–66.

Kenneth G. Zysk, 'Religious Healing in the Veda', *Transactions of the American Philosophical Society*, N.S. 75, 7 (1985): 1–311.

Maurice Bloomfield, *Hymns of the Atharva-Veda* (Oxford, 1897), p. 163.

Quote regarding 'childish' Atharvaveda from Om Prakash, *Cultural History of India* (New Delhi, 2005), p. 96.

Michel Strickmann, 'The Consecration Sūtra: A Buddhist Book of Spells', in Robert E. Buswell, Jr (ed.), *Chinese Buddhist Apocrypha* (Honolulu, 1990), pp. 75–119; Christine Mollier, *Buddhism and Taoism Face to Face: Scripture, Ritual, and Iconographic Exchange in Medieval China* (Honolulu, 2008), chapter 2.

Marvin Meyer, 'The Prayer of Mary Who Dissolves Chains in Coptic Magic and Religion', in Paul Allan Mirecki and Marvin W. Meyer (eds.), *Magic and Ritual in the Ancient World* (Leiden, 2002), pp. 407–16.

Joshua Trachtenberg, *Jewish Magic and Superstition: A Study in Folk Religion* (New York, 1939).

On the Bible as an amulet, see Jean Vezin, 'Les livres utilises comme amulettes et comme reliques', in Peter Ganz (ed.), *Das Buch als Magisches und als Repräsentationsobjekt* (Wiesbaden, 1992), pp. 101–15.

W. L. Hildburgh, 'Notes on Some Amulets of the Three Magi Kings', *Folklore*, 19, 1 (1908): 83–7.

Don C. Skemer, *Binding Words: Textual Amulets in the Middle Ages* (University Park, 2006), pp. 96–105.

Marduk charm cited in Erica Reiner, 'Plague Amulets and House Blessings', *Journal of Near Eastern Studies*, 19, 2 (1960): 151.

Carol Andrews, *Amulets of Ancient Egypt* (Austin, 1994).

Donaldson, 'Koran as Magic' and Kathleen Malone O'Connor, 'Popular and Talismanic Uses of the Qur'ān', in Jane Dammen McAuliffe (ed.), *Encyclopaedia of the Qur'ān* (Leiden, 2004), vol. 4, pp. 168–81.

David Owusu-Ansah, *Islamic Talismanic Tradition in Nineteenth-Century Asante* (Lewiston, 1991).

R. Orme-Smith, 'Maiduguri Market – Northern Nigeria', *African Affairs* (1938): 323.

O. A. Adekunle, O. I. Oladele, and T. D. Olukaiyeja, 'Indigenous Control Methods for Pests and Diseases of Cattle in Northern Nigeria', *Livestock Research for Rural Development*, 14, 2 (2002).

Daniel A. Offiong, 'Witchcraft among the Ibibio of Nigeria', *African Studies Review*, 26, 1 (1983): 121.

On Delaurence, see Davies, *Grimoires*, pp. 215–31.

On *mezuzahs*, see Eva-Maria Jansson, *The Message of a Mitsvah: The Mezuzah in Rabbinic Literature* (1999); Bohak, *Ancient Jewish Magic*, p. 67; Trachtenberg, *Jewish Magic and Superstition*.

Eli Davis, 'The Psalms in Hebrew Medical Amulets', *Vetus Testamentum*, 42, 2 (1992): 173–8.

On the Nachman formula, see Maureen Bloom, *Jewish Mysticism and Magic: An Anthropological Perspective* (London, 2007), p. 29.

On Arabic letter magic, see Annemarie Schimmel, *Deciphering the Signs of God: A Phenomenological Approach to Islam* (Albany, 1994), chapter 4; Mushegh Asatrian, 'Ibn Khaldūn on Magic and the Occult', *Iran and the Caucasus*, 7, 1–2 (2003): 73–123; Amber B. Gemmeke, *Marabout Women in Dakar: Creating Trust in a Rural Urban Space* (Berlin, 2008), p. 16.

The library on Kabbalah is very large and variable in quality. The classic text is Gershom Scholem, *Origins of the Kabbalah*, tr. Allan Arkush (Philadelphia, 1987). Good introductions are Joseph Dan, *A Very Short Introduction to the Kabbalah* (Oxford, 2007); Hava Tirosh-Samuelson, 'Jewish Mysticism', in Judith R. Baskin and Kenneth Seeskin (eds.), *The Cambridge Guide to Jewish History, Religion, and Culture* (Cambridge, 2010), chapter 16.

Davies, *Grimoires.*

On Chinese magic texts, see Mu-Chou Poo, 'Popular Religion in Pre-Imperial China: Observations on the Almanacs of Shui-hu-ti', *T'oung Pao*, 79 (1993): 225–48; Donald Harper, 'A Chinese Demonography of the Third Century BC', *Harvard Journal of Asiatic Studies*, 45, 2 (1985): 459–98; Donald Harper, 'Warring States Natural Philosophy and Occult Thought', in Michael Loewe and Edward L. Shaughnessy (eds.), *The Cambridge History of Ancient China* (Cambridge, 1999), chapter 12.

Chapter 5

Clay ball charm examples in Ja 'Far Sharif, Gerhard Andreas Herklots, and William Crooke, *Islam in India* (London, 1921), p. 275; George Lyman Kittredge, *Witchcraft in Old and New England* (New York, 1958), pp. 192–3.

Quote on magical mimesis from Michael Taussig, *Mimesis and Alterity: A Particular History of the Senses* (New York, 1993), p. 57.

Steven M. Oberhelman, *Dreambooks in Byzantium* (Aldershot, 2008).

Harlan I. Smith, 'Sympathetic Magic and Witchcraft among the Bellacoola', *American Anthropologist*, N.S. 27, 1 (1925): 116–21.

Jürgen Wasim Frembgen, 'The Scorpion in Muslim Folklore', *Asian Folklore Studies*, 63, 1 (2004): 95–123.

James D. Keyser and David S. Whitley, 'Sympathetic Magic in Western North American Rock Art', *American Antiquity*, 71, 1 (2006): 3–26.

William E. Welmers, 'Secret Medicines, Magic, and Rites of the Kpelle Tribe in Liberia', *Southwestern Journal of Anthropology*, 5, 3 (1949): 216.

On the transference of illness, see Wayland D. Hand, *Magical Medicine: The Folkloric Component of Medicine in the Folk Belief, Custom, and Ritual of the Peoples of Europe and America* (Berkeley, 1980); Owen Davies, 'European Folk Medicine', in Stephen B. Kayne (ed.), *Traditional Medicine: A Global Perspective* (London, 2009), pp. 25–44.

On Amadou Bamba, see G. Wesley Johnson, *The Emergence of Black Politics in Senegal* (Stanford, 1971), pp. 126–7; Leonardo Alfonso Villalón, *Islamic Society and State Power in Senegal* (Cambridge, 1995), pp. 121–3.

J. J. M. De Groot, *The Religious System of China* (Leiden, 1910), vol. 6, pp. 1244–5.

For a global comparison of female magicians, see Hutton Webster, *Magic: A Sociological Study* (Stanford, 1948), chapter 7.

Amber B. Gemmeke, *Marabout Women in Dakar: Creating Trust in a Rural Urban Space* (Berlin, 2008).

Georg Zimmermann quoted in Robert Scribner, *Religion and Culture in Germany (1400–1800)*, ed. Lyndal Roper (Leiden, 2001), p. 324.

William Brewer letters quoted in Owen Davies, *A People Bewitched* (Bruton, 1999), pp. 70–3.

On Jinns in different Islamic cultures, see, for example, Ja 'Far Sharif, Gerhard Andreas Herklots, and William Crooke, *Islam in India* (London, 1921); Moiz Ansari, *Islam and the Paranormal* (Lincoln, NE, 2006).

Larry G. Peters, 'Trance, Initiation, and Psychotherapy in Tamang Shamanism', *American Ethnologist* (1982), vol. 9, 1 (1982), pp. 21-46.

Alexandre Popovic, 'Magic among the Balkan Populations: Convergences and Divergences', *Balkanologie*, 8, 2 (2004).

On the etymology of fetishism, see Peter Melville Logan, *Victorian Fetishism: Intellectuals and Primitives* (Albany, 2009); Roy Ellen, 'Fetishism', *Man*, N.S. 23 (1988): 213–35; David Murray, *Matter, Magic, and Spirit: Representing Indian and African American Belief* (Philadelphia, 2006).

Michael T. Taussig, *The Nervous System* (London, 1992), chapter 7.

On magic in museum collections, see Mary Bouquet and Nuno Porto (eds.), *Science, Magic and Religion: The Ritual Processes of Museum Magic* (New York, 2005). For an important analysis of

Scottish collections, see Hugh Cheape, '"Charms against Witchcraft": Magic and Mischief in Museum Collections', in Julian Goodare, Lauren Martin, and Joyce Miller (eds.), *Witchcraft and Belief in Early Modern Scotland* (Basingstoke, 2008), chapter 10.

Chapter 6

On modernity and enchantment, see Simon During, *Modern Enchantments* (Cambridge, Mass., 2002); Michael Saler, 'Modernity and Enchantment: A Historiographic Review', *American Historical Review*, 111 (2006): 692–716; Randall Styers, *Making Magic*; Alex Owen, *The Place of Enchantment: British Occultism and the Culture of the Modern* (Chicago, 2004); Birgit Meyer and Peter Pels (eds.), *Magic and Modernity: Interfaces of Revelation and Concealment* (Stanford, 2003).

The idea of a 'crisis of evidence' is discussed in Peter Lamont, 'Spiritualism and a Mid-Victorian Crisis of Evidence', *Historical Journal*, 47, 4 (2004): 897–920.

On the telegraph and spiritualism, see Jeffrey Sconce, *Haunted Media: Electronic Presence from Telegraph to Television* (Durham, NC, 2000); Pamela Thurschwell, *Literature, Technology, and Magical Thinking*, 1880–1920 (Cambridge, 2001); Richard Noakes, 'Cromwell Varley FRS, Electrical Discharge and Victorian Spiritualism', *Notes and Records of the Royal Society of London*, 61 (2005): 5–22.

On the 'crisis of faith', see Herbert Schlossberg, *Conflict and Crisis in the Religious Life of Late Victorian England* (New Brunswick, 2009).

On the development of modern British magic, see Ronald Hutton, *The Triumph of the Moon: A History of Modern Pagan Witchcraft* (Oxford, 1999); Alison Butler, *Victorian Occultism and the Making of Modern Magic* (Basingstoke, 2011).

Max Ernst quoted in Alyce Mahon, 'The Search for a New Dimension: Surrealism and Magic', in Amy Wygant (ed.), *The Meanings of Magic: From the Bible to Buffalo Bill* (New York, 2006), p. 221.

Julien Leiris quoted in Christopher Green, *Picasso: Architecture and Vertigo* (New Haven, 2005), p. 199.

Tolkien quoted in Patrick Curry, 'Magic vs. Enchantment', *Journal of Contemporary Religion*, 14, 3 (1999): 401.

Davies, *A People Bewitched*, pp. 162–3.

Heike Behrend, 'Photo Magic: Photographs in Practices of Healing and Harming in East Africa', *Journal of Religion in Africa*, 33, 2 (2003): 129–45.
Frank C. Brown, *Frank C. Brown Collection of North Carolina Folklore* (Durham, 1964), pp. 109–10.
Gabriel Klaeger, 'Religion on the Road: The Spiritual Experience of Road Travel in Ghana', in Jan-Bart Gewald, Sabine Luning, and Klaas van Walraven (eds.), *The Speed of Change: Motor Vehicles and People in Africa, 1890–2000* (Leiden, 2009), chapter 9.
Daniel Jordan Smith, 'Cell Phones, Social Inequality, and Contemporary Culture in Nigeria', *Canadian Journal of African Studies*, 40, 3 (2006): 496–7.
R. Serge Denisoff and William L. Schurk, *Tarnished Gold: The Record Industry Revisited* (New Brunswick, 1986), chapter 8.
Richard Stivers, *Technology as Magic: The Triumph of the Irrational* (New York, 1999), chapter 4; Linda Dégh, *American Folklore and the Mass Media* (Bloomington, 1994), chapter 2; James B. Twitchell, *Lead Us into Temptation: The Triumph of American Materialism* (New York, 1999), pp. 50–90.
On magical thinking in children, see Eugene Subbotsky, *Magic and the Mind: Mechanisms, Functions, and Development of Magical Thinking and Behaviour* (Oxford, 2010); Leonard Zusne and Warren H. Jones, *Anomalistic Psychology: A Study of Magical Thinking* (Hillsdale, 1989); Jacqueline D. Woolley, Katrina E. Phelps, Debra L. Davis, and Dorothy J. Mandell, 'Where Theories of Mind Meet Magic: The Development of Children's Beliefs about Wishing', *Child Development*, 70, 3 (1999): 571–87.
Sylvia Anthony, *The Child's Discovery of Death* (London, 1940), p. 171.
Deborah J. Taub and Heather L. Servaty-Seib, 'Controversial Content: Is Harry Potter Harmful to Children?', in Elizabeth E. Heilman (ed.), *Critical Perspectives on Harry Potter*, 2nd edn. (New York, 2009), chapter 1.
Laura M. Simonds, James D. Demetre, and Cristina Read, 'Relationships between Magical Thinking, Obsessive-Compulsiveness and Other Forms of Anxiety in a Sample of Non-Clinical Children', *Developmental Psychology*, 27, 2 (2009): 457–71.
A brief introduction of cognitive theory with regard to religion can be found in Cunningham, *Religion and Magic*. A detailed theoretical account is provided in Sørensen, *A Cognitive Theory of Magic*. More generally, on the theory of mind and folk psychology, see

Daniel Hutto, *Folk Psychological Narratives: The Socio-Cultural Basis of Understanding Reasons* (Cambridge, Mass., 2008).

On the theory of 'thing using', see F. T. Evans, 'Two Legs, Thing Using and Talking: The Origins of the Creative Engineering Mind', in Satinder P. Gill (ed.), *Cognition, Communication and Interaction: Transdiciplinary Perspectives on Interactive Technology* (2008), p. 324.

István Czachesz, 'Magic and Mind: Toward a New Cognitive Theory of Magic, with Special Attention to the Canonical and Apocryphal Acts of the Apostles', in T. Nicklas and Th. J. Kraus (eds.), *Neues Testament und Magie: Verhältnisbestimmungen*, special issue of *Annali di Storia dell'Esegesi*, 24 (2007): 295–321.

Ed Bever, *The Realities of Witchcraft and Popular Magic in Early Modern Europe: Culture, Cognition, and Everyday Life* (Basingstoke, 2008). For a range of critical assessments of Bever's approach, see the journal *Magic, Ritual, and Witchcraft*, 5, 1 (2010): 81–122.

Susan Greenwood, *The Nature of Magic: An Anthropology of Consciousness* (Oxford, 2005).

Ariel Glucklich, *The End of Magic* (Oxford, 1997), p. 13.

Further reading

For general surveys of the meaning of magic in a European context, see Michael D. Bailey, *Magic and Superstition in Europe: A Concise History from Antiquity to the Present* (Lanham, 2007) and Robert Ralley, *Magic: A Beginner's Guide* (Oxford, 2010). Popular magical traditions in Europe are explored in Keith Thomas, *Religion and the Decline of Magic* (London, 1971); Stephen Wilson, *The Magical Universe: Everyday Ritual and Magic in Pre-Modern Europe* (London, 2000); Owen Davies, *Popular Magic: Cunning-Folk in English History* (London, 2007). On magic and the notion of superstition, see Euan Cameron, *Enchanted Europe: Superstition, Reason, and Religion 1250–1750* (Oxford, 2010). On medieval Europe, see Valerie Flint, *The Rise of Magic in Early Medieval Europe* (Princeton, 1991) and Richard Kieckhefer, *Magic in the Middle Ages* (Cambridge, 1989). The esoteric tradition is traced in B. J. Gibbons, *Spirituality and the Occult: From the Renaissance to the Modern Age* (London, 2001) and Nicholas Goodrick-Clarke, *The Western Esoteric Traditions: A Historical Introduction* (Oxford, 2008).

Magic in antiquity is explained in Matthew Dickie, *Magic and Magicians in the Greco-Roman World* (London, 2001); Daniel Ogden, *Magic, Witchcraft, and Ghosts in the Greek and Roman World: A Sourcebook* (Oxford, 2002); Geraldine Pinch, *Magic in Ancient Egypt* (Austin, 1994); Rosalie David, *Religion and Magic in Ancient Egypt* (London, 2002); Gideon Bohak, *Ancient Jewish Magic: A History* (Cambridge, 2008). Early Arabic and Islamic magic is explored in Emilie Savage-Smith (ed.), *Magic and Divination in Early Islam* (Aldershot, 2004).

On books of magic, see Owen Davies, *Grimoires: A History of Magic Books* (Oxford, 2009); Sophie Page, *Magic in Medieval Manuscripts* (London, 2004); Benedek Lang, *Manuscripts of Learned Magic in the Medieval Libraries of Central Europe* (Philadelphia, 2008); Richard Kieckhefer, *Forbidden Rites: A Necromancer's Manual of the Fifteenth Century* (Stroud, 1997).

For a flavour of magical traditions around the globe, and how they have been represented, try Robert A. Voeks, *Sacred Leaves of Candomblé: African Magic, Medicine, and Religion in Brazil* (Austin, 1997); David Murray, *Matter, Magic, and Spirit: Representing Indian and African American Belief* (Philadelphia, 2007); Ronald Hutton, *Shamans: Siberian Spirituality and the Western Imagination* (London, 2007); Jane DeBernardi, *Chinese Popular Religion and Spirit Mediums in Penang, Malaysia* (Stanford, 2006); Lee Siegel, *Net of Magic: Wonders and Deceptions in India* (Chicago, 1991).

Brief introductions to the debates regarding the anthropology of religion, magic, and science are provided in Graham Cunningham, *Religion and Magic: Approaches and Theories* (Edinburgh, 1999), and Rebecca L. Stein and Philip L. Stein, *The Anthropology of Religion, Magic, and Witchcraft*, 2nd edn. (Boston, 2008). For more depth, see Randall Styers, *Making Magic: Religion, Magic and Science in the Modern World* (Oxford, 2004).

Magical practice and modernity is explored in Ronald Hutton, *The Triumph of the Moon: A History of Modern Pagan Witchcraft* (Oxford, 1999); Alison Butler, *Victorian Occultism and the Making of Modern Magic* (Basingstoke, 2011); Susan Greenwood, *The Nature of Magic: An Anthropology of Consciousness* (Oxford, 2005); Alex Owen, *The Place of Enchantment: British Occultism and the Culture of the Modern* (Chicago, 2004).

Index

A

Abduh, Mohammed 9
abracadabra 74
Adam 36
advertising 106
Ady, Thomas 51, 54, 56
Africa 6, 12, 22, 23, 41, 57, 72
Agrippa, Cornelius 45, 80
Ahura Mazda 3
al-Bāqillānī 51
Albertus Magnus 80
al-Buni, Ahmed bin Ali 80
Algeria 57
Al-Suyútí 67, 81
America 25, 73, 86, 94, 106
Amnesty International 11
amulets 4, 69–78, 97
Andaman Islands 22
angels 34
animal magnetism 37–8
animism 15, 61
apocrypha 70–1
Aristotle 32
art 101
  objects 97
  rock 86
Atharvaveda 68–9, 79
Augustine of Hippo 42
Australia 17, 22, 86

B

Bacon, Roger 42, 80
Bamba, Amadou 88–9
Bektanis 33
Bible 4, 5, 48, 51, 66, 70–1, 73, 89
Blavatsky, Helena Petrovna 40
blood 6, 92
Blum, Eva and Richard 29
Bolus of Mendes 33
Bosnia 94
Breton, André 101
Brewer, William 91
Britten, Emma Hardinge 40
Bruno, Giordano 45

C

camera 104
camera obscura 55
Canada 85
Catholicism 40, 46, 89
Charcot, Jean-Martin 59, 61
Cheiromecta 33
China 39, 69, 79, 90
Christianity 6, 7, 14, 34, 43, 70–1
Church, the 4, 6, 41, 43
Clark, Stuart 45
Clementine, Bishop 33

Crowley, Aleister 103
cunning folk 91–2, 97

D

Darfur 67
Darwin, Charles 15
Dee, John 45
De Martino, Ernesto 30
Democritus 33
Denmark 44
Devil, *see* Satan
dhāranī-sūtras 69, 79
Dioscorides 85
disenchantment 46–7
djinns 67, 92–3
Douglas, Mary 20
dreams 85, 106
Durkheim, Émile 17–18, 110

E

Egypt 9, 10
electricity 104
England 44, 47
Ennemoser, Joseph 38–9, 40, 87
Epicurus 50
Epiphanius 34
erasure 68
ergot 58
Ernst, Max 101
Erra 71
Eudoxus 32
Evans-Pritchard, E.E. 22–23, 25, 29
evil eye 28, 68, 77

F

fairies 92, 97
fakis 67
familiars 53
Favret-Saada, Jeanne 31
fetish 95–6
Ficino, Marsilio 45
Finland 28
folklorists 29
Foster, George 27
Fourie, Louis 41
France 31, 57, 59, 81, 101, 105
Frazer, James 16–17, 62, 83, 86
Freemasonry 37, 101
Freud, Sigmund 60–3

G

Galen 85
Gennep, Arnold van 19
Germany 6, 31, 101
Ghana 105
goeteia 2
Golden Dawn 101, 103
Greece 29
  ancient 2–3, 49
grimoires 78–81; *see also* magic books
Guinea 72, 95

H

Ham 34
Hamesh 77
Hamsa 77
Hand of Fatima 77
Hand of Miriam 77
Hastings, Warren 37
Hegel, G.W.F. 14
Hellebore 58, 59
Hermes Trismegistus 35, 40
Herodotus 3
Hinduism 8
Hippocrates 49
Hopkins, Mathew 53
horseshoe 9
Houdin, Jean-Eugène Robert 57
Houdini 57
Howitt, William 38
Hungary 92

I

illusion 50–57
India 8, 37, 38, 40, 57, 68, 112
Ireland 97
Islam 6, 7–8, 42, 66–8, 92–3
Israel 74
Italy 28, 30, 92

J

Jahoda, Gustav 63
Jesus 5
Judaism 6, 33–4, 42, 73–4, 75–7
juggling 51–2, 56

K

Kabbalah 37, 40, 75–7
Kemal, Mustafa 8
Kenya 104
Khaldūn, Ibn 50, 75
Kieckhefer, Richard 43
Koran 10, 66–8, 72–3, 75, 81, 89, 90, 93, 94
Kuan-ting ching 69
Kyrgyzstan 11

L

Lang, Andrew 17
Leiris, Julien 101
Leon, Moshe de 76
Lévi, Éliphas 39–40
Liberia 87
Liminality 19
Limited Good, theory of 27–8
Lucian 49

M

magic, magical
  and evolutionary models 15–16
  and gender 90, 92
  and religion 15–19, 26
  and science 17, 41–3
  and technology 103–6
  as popular religion 8–13, 79, 94
  as symbolic construction 19–21, 22, 30
  books 78–81
  contagious 86–7, 110
  execution for practising 11
  goetic 36
  lantern 55
  linguistic origin 2
  literary 67–81; *see also* grimoires
  'Mosoaicall' 36
  natural 5, 36, 42, 55
  optical 54
  practitioners of 29, 49–50, 88–95; *see also* cunning folk; marabouts
  Roman 4
  scepticism regarding 50
  sympathetic 83
  theurgic 36
  transference of disease 87–8
magi (New Testament) 5
magical thinking 63, 106–12
  children 107–9
magical world view 25–7, 30
magico-religious 18
magoi, magos 2–3, 4
Malinowski, Bronisław 22, 26, 41, 63
Mana 27
Manu, Law Code of 39
marabouts 8, 57, 75, 88, 90
Marx, Karl 14–15
material culture 95–8
mathematics 45
Mauss, Marcel 18, 84
melancholy 59
Mesmer, Franz Anton 37–8
Mesraim 34
mezuzah 73
mobile phones 105
Montaigne, Michel de 58

Moses 34, 70
Mowinckel, Sigmund 26

N

Nachman, Rabbi 75
narcotics 58
Naudé, Gabriel 35–6
necromancy 2
Nectanebus 33
Neoplatonism 44, 77
Nepal 93
New Guinea 93
Newton, Isaac 45
Nigeria 72, 73, 105
Nimrod 34
Noah 34

O

obsessive compulsive disorder 64
onni 28
Origen 5
Osthanes 33

P

paganism 9, 99
Papua New Guinea 22
papyrus 78
Persia, Persians 2, 3, 4, 32, 94
photography 104–5
Piaget, Jean 63, 107
Pitt-Rivers, Julian 29
Pliny the Elder 4, 32, 33
pollution 20
Porta, Giambattista della 54–5, 58
Potter, Harry 108
Protestantism 46–7, 89
Pseudo-Clementines 33
psychiatry 58–63, 107–10
psychology 63–5
Puerto Rico 13

R

Radcliffe-Brown, A.R. 22
Rannie, John 56
Ravensburg, Simon 35
Redfield, Robert 26
Reformation 47, 50
religion
  folk/popular 8–13
  syncretic 12
ringworm 21
Róheim, Géza 62

S

sai kong 90
Samuel 51
Satan 36, 43, 51, 59, 67
Saraswati, Swami Dayanand 8
Saudi Arabia 11
Saul, King 51
Schmidt, Wilhelm 18
Schöck, Inge 31
Scot, Reginald 51, 52–3, 56
Scotland 44, 97
Sebald, Hans 31
shamanism 93–4
signatures, doctrine of 85
sihr 9, 11, 66–7
shirk 9, 66
Simon Magus 34, 54, 70
Solomon 34, 70, 80, 93
Solomon's Mountain 11
Sophoclese 3
sorcery 25, 61
Spain 29, 94
Spencer, Herbert 15
spiritualism 38, 100
Subbotsky, Eugene 107
Sufism 7, 67, 75, 90
superstition 41–2, 63–5
Surrealism 101

T

Talmud 66
Tambiah, Stanley 20
tarot cards 101
Tertullian of Carthage 4
Thomas, Keith 47
Thorndike, Lynn 43
Tolkien, J.R.R. 103
Torah 70, 74, 75
Trobriand Islands 22, 41
Turkey 8
Tylor, Edward Burnett 15–16, 62, 83

V

Varley, Cromwell 100
Vaughan, Thomas 36
ventriloquism 54
Virgin Mary 70
vodou/voodoo 12, 65

W

Wahhabi movement 7, 67
Warburg, John Cimon 102
wasp 4
Wax, Rosalie and Murray 25–6
Weber, Max 6, 46–7
Weyer, Johann 54, 58, 59
Wilkins, John 45
witch bottle 97–8
witchcraft 44, 53, 58–9, 61, 65, 91, 92, 105
Witch of Endor 51, 54
Wittgenstein, Ludwig 20, 22

Xerxes 3, 33

Y

Yeats, W.B. 99–100, 101

Z

Zande 23, 25
Zimmermann, Georg 91
Zoroaster, Zoroastrianism 3, 32, 33, 34, 39
Zwemer, Samuel Marinus 6

Expand your collection of
VERY SHORT INTRODUCTIONS

1. Classics
2. Music
3. Buddhism
4. Literary Theory
5. Hinduism
6. Psychology
7. Islam
8. Politics
9. Theology
10. Archaeology
11. Judaism
12. Sociology
13. The Koran
14. The Bible
15. Social and Cultural Anthropology
16. History
17. Roman Britain
18. The Anglo-Saxon Age
19. Medieval Britain
20. The Tudors
21. Stuart Britain
22. Eighteenth-Century Britain
23. Nineteenth-Century Britain
24. Twentieth-Century Britain
25. Heidegger
26. Ancient Philosophy
27. Socrates
28. Marx
29. Logic
30. Descartes
31. Machiavelli
32. Aristotle
33. Hume
34. Nietzsche
35. Darwin
36. The European Union
37. Gandhi
38. Augustine
39. Intelligence
40. Jung
41. Buddha
42. Paul
43. Continental Philosophy
44. Galileo
45. Freud
46. Wittgenstein
47. Indian Philosophy
48. Rousseau
49. Hegel
50. Kant
51. Cosmology
52. Drugs
53. Russian Literature
54. The French Revolution
55. Philosophy
56. Barthes
57. Animal Rights
58. Kierkegaard
59. Russell
60. Shakespeare
61. Clausewitz
62. Schopenhauer
63. The Russian Revolution
64. Hobbes
65. World Music
66. Mathematics
67. Philosophy of Science
68. Cryptography
69. Quantum Theory
70. Spinoza
71. Choice Theory
72. Architecture
73. Poststructuralism

74. Postmodernism
75. Democracy
76. Empire
77. Fascism
78. Terrorism
79. Plato
80. Ethics
81. Emotion
82. Northern Ireland
83. Art Theory
84. Locke
85. Modern Ireland
86. Globalization
87. The Cold War
88. The History of Astronomy
89. Schizophrenia
90. The Earth
91. Engels
92. British Politics
93. Linguistics
94. The Celts
95. Ideology
96. Prehistory
97. Political Philosophy
98. Postcolonialism
99. Atheism
100. Evolution
101. Molecules
102. Art History
103. Presocratic Philosophy
104. The Elements
105. Dada and Surrealism
106. Egyptian Myth
107. Christian Art
108. Capitalism
109. Particle Physics
110. Free Will
111. Myth
112. Ancient Egypt
113. Hieroglyphs
114. Medical Ethics
115. Kafka
116. Anarchism
117. Ancient Warfare
118. Global Warming
119. Christianity
120. Modern Art
121. Consciousness
122. Foucault
123. The Spanish Civil War
124. The Marquis de Sade
125. Habermas
126. Socialism
127. Dreaming
128. Dinosaurs
129. Renaissance Art
130. Buddhist Ethics
131. Tragedy
132. Sikhism
133. The History of Time
134. Nationalism
135. The World Trade Organization
136. Design
137. The Vikings
138. Fossils
139. Journalism
140. The Crusades
141. Feminism
142. Human Evolution
143. The Dead Sea Scrolls
144. The Brain
145. Global Catastrophes
146. Contemporary Art
147. Philosophy of Law
148. The Renaissance
149. Anglicanism
150. The Roman Empire
151. Photography
152. Psychiatry
153. Existentialism
154. The First World War
155. Fundamentalism
156. Economics
157. International Migration
158. Newton
159. Chaos

160. African History
161. Racism
162. Kabbalah
163. Human Rights
164. International Relations
165. The American Presidency
166. The Great Depression and The New Deal
167. Classical Mythology
168. The New Testament as Literature
169. American Political Parties and Elections
170. Bestsellers
171. Geopolitics
172. Antisemitism
173. Game Theory
174. HIV/AIDS
175. Documentary Film
176. Modern China
177. The Quakers
178. German Literature
179. Nuclear Weapons
180. Law
181. The Old Testament
182. Galaxies
183. Mormonism
184. Religion in America
185. Geography
186. The Meaning of Life
187. Sexuality
188. Nelson Mandela
189. Science and Religion
190. Relativity
191. The History of Medicine
192. Citizenship
193. The History of Life
194. Memory
195. Autism
196. Statistics
197. Scotland
198. Catholicism
199. The United Nations
200. Free Speech
201. The Apocryphal Gospels
202. Modern Japan
203. Lincoln
204. Superconductivity
205. Nothing
206. Biography
207. The Soviet Union
208. Writing and Script
209. Communism
210. Fashion
211. Forensic Science
212. Puritanism
213. The Reformation
214. Thomas Aquinas
215. Deserts
216. The Norman Conquest
217. Biblical Archaeology
218. The Reagan Revolution
219. The Book of Mormon
220. Islamic History
221. Privacy
222. Neoliberalism
223. Progressivism
224. Epidemiology
225. Information
226. The Laws of Thermodynamics
227. Innovation
228. Witchcraft
229. The New Testament
230. French Literature
231. Film Music
232. Druids
233. German Philosophy
234. Advertising
235. Forensic Psychology
236. Modernism
237. Leadership
238. Christian Ethics
239. Tocqueville
240. Landscapes and Geomorphology
241. Spanish Literature

242. Diplomacy
243. North American Indians
244. The U.S. Congress
245. Romanticism
246. Utopianism
247. The Blues
248. Keynes
249. English Literature
250. Agnosticism
251. Aristocracy
252. Martin Luther
253. Michael Faraday
254. Planets
255. Pentecostalism
256. Humanism
257. Folk Music
258. Late Antiquity
259. Genius
260. Numbers
261. Muhammad
262. Beauty
263. Critical Theory
264. Organizations
265. Early Music
266. The Scientific Revolution
267. Cancer
268. Nuclear Power
269. Paganism
270. Risk
271. Science Fiction
272. Herodotus
273. Conscience
274. American Immigration
275. Jesus
276. Viruses
277. Protestantism
278. Derrida
279. Madness
280. Developmental Biology
281. Dictionaries
282. Global Economic History
283. Multiculturalism
284. Environmental Economics
285. The Cell
286. Ancient Greece
287. Angels
288. Children's Literature
289. The Periodic Table
290. Modern France
291. Reality
292. The Computer
293. The Animal Kingdom
294. Colonial Latin American Literature
295. Sleep
296. The Aztecs
297. The Cultural Revolution
298. Modern Latin American Literature
299. Magic

PAGANISM

A Very Short Introduction

Owen Davies

This *Very Short Introduction* explores the meaning of paganism - through a chronological overview of the attitudes towards its practices and beliefs - from the ancient world through to the present day. Owen Davies largely looks at paganism through the eyes of the Christian world, and how, over the centuries, notions and representations of its nature were shaped by religious conflict, power struggles, colonialism, and scholarship. Despite the expansion of Christianity and Islam, Pagan cultures continue to exist around the world, whilst in the West new formations of paganism constitute one of the fastest-growing religions.

www.oup.com/vsi

ONLINE CATALOGUE

A Very Short Introduction

Our online catalogue is designed to make it easy to find your ideal Very Short Introduction. View the entire collection by subject area, watch author videos, read sample chapters, and download reading guides.

SOCIAL MEDIA
Very Short Introduction

Join our community

www.oup.com/vsi

- Join us online at the official Very Short Introductions **Facebook** page.
- Access the thoughts and musings of our authors with our online **blog**.
- Sign up for our monthly **e-newsletter** to receive information on all new titles publishing that month.
- Browse the full range of Very Short Introductions online.
- Read **extracts** from the Introductions for free.
- Visit our library of **Reading Guides**. These guides, written by our expert authors will help you to question again, why you think what you think.
- If you are a teacher or lecturer you can order inspection copies quickly and simply via our website.